GOLF IN A NUTSHELL

GOLF IN A NUTSHELL

The Flight of the Ball Tells it All

JOHN JACOBS
and
PETER DOBEREINER

Hodder & Stoughton

First published in 1995 by Hodder and Stoughton
A division of Hodder Headline PLC

10 9 8 7 6 5 4 3 2 1

British Library Cataloguing in Publication Data

Jacobs, John
Golf in a Nutshell
I. Title II. Dobereiner, Peter
796.352

ISBN 0 340 63988 1

Typeset by Palimpsest Book Production Limited,
Polmont, Stirlingshire
Printed and bound in Great Britain by
Mackays of Chatham PLC, Chatham, Kent

Hodder and Stoughton
A division of Hodder Headline PLC
338 Euston Road
London NW1 3BH

CONTENTS

THE ETERNAL FUNDAMENTALS

THE BACK NINE

ACKNOWLEDGMENTS

In *Golf in a Nutshell*, I have, yet again, been fortunate to work with a co-author whose writing I have always admired. It has made the whole venture not a work but a pleasure. But then, Peter Dobereiner's own books have given me such pleasure over the years and I have anticipated and devoured his articles in the golfing magazines with the same satisfaction and delight. For a good while I even changed my daily paper in order not to be deprived of his weekly perspicacity and unique turn of phrase.

The reflections I gave Peter were mostly anecdotal and hotchpotch. He has dealt with them bravely for reflections are, after all, blinks of the memory and not easy to capture on paper. That he has managed to do so in the best Dobereiner tradition, yet allowing my own voice to ring through is, I feel, a rare achievement. He has my grateful thanks for pulling it off.

As has happened before, my publisher, Roddy Bloomfield, has been the spur that prompted me to undertake this book

We have worked happily together for 25 years and I cannot let the occasion pass without acknowledging the debt of gratitude I owe him.

I was so lucky to be taken on by someone with as keen a love of the game as myself. It has made such a difference, and I am happy to report that Roddy's golf has improved.

I am also deeply grateful to those friends who have been kind enough to wish this book Godspeed by writing introductory notes. In my lifetime I have given lessons and advice to thousands of people but that giving, as I have tried to explain in this book, is a two-way process. For every gift of golfing help I have been able to dispense, I have been rewarded many thousandfold because each individual has reciprocated with gifts of gratitude, appreciation and, above all, friendship. You may judge the measure of this treasury of friendship by the words which follow, from Michael Bonallack, Gary Player, Bernard Gallacher, José Maria Olazabal, Mickey Walker and Dave Marr.

John Jacobs.

TRIBUTES

From Michael Bonallack

In 1971 I was fortunate to be the Captain of Great Britain and Ireland Walker Cup team playing against the United States of America on the Old Course at St Andrews, a match which we won for only the second time, the first being in 1938.

The success of the team was in no small measure due to the fact that John Jacobs had been involved with the team's preparation, and was also present throughout the whole week, giving help where needed to those whose game was not quite up to scratch and at the same time building up the confidence of the team as a whole.

John knows so much about the game that realising it is not possible to make drastic swing alterations he was able to improve everyone's game by giving them one thought on which to focus, his expertise enabling him to pick out a different thought for each player.

Only last year whilst in America I had my first lesson for years from John Geering at Sea Island who told me my set-up was completely wrong and who put me in a position from which he told me I would be able to hit a ball in the back, whereupon I remarked that the last time anybody said a similar thing to me was about 20 years ago and that was John Jacobs. At this John Geering beamed and said, 'I am a John Jacobs disciple.' Maybe that is why he has such a good reputation as a teacher.

From Bernard Gallacher

When I first saw John Jacobs I had no idea that, although from different generations, we would become such good friends. I was just 14 at the time and more enthusiastic about golf than anything else in the world. John whom people forget was a better than useful player in his day, was on the practice range at Dalmahoy, one of my clubs and venue of the old Senior Service tournament.

It was not his swing that caught my eye or the way he addressed the ball but rather the fact that he never had time to practise himself because so many of his colleagues kept asking for advice.

As always it was freely given. I doubt whether any other player has given of his time and expertise as much as John whose ability to analyse swings, spot errors and correct faults has always been second to none.

Quirky new methods have become all the rage from time to time but John has always preached and practised the same tried and trusted method for 40 years . . . and, take my word for it, it is the correct method.

He told me when I was a headstrong 16-year-old that I could not progress as far as I would want to unless I changed my grip. I felt I was doing well enough and refused to change. Years later I did as he had suggested and only wished I had done it sooner!

John remains the supreme enthusiast gaining his pleasure in golf from helping fellow pros and amateurs – thousands over the years – play the game better and enjoy it more.

Yet while his reputation as a coach is legendary worldwide – his *Practical Golf* instruction book, one of many he has produced, has been a best-seller in various languages for years – he has been a *tour de force* behind the scenes in professional golf.

It was his expertise, his knowledge of the European scene as coach to most of the national sides, which was invaluable when it came to setting up and co-ordinating the PGA European Tour in the early '70s with the various Continental Federations. He was the man for the job and look what Ken Schofield, John's hand-picked successor, has achieved with the Volvo Tour since.

Loyalty, honesty and integrity are readily associated with John Jacobs who was a man ahead of his time when he pioneered driving ranges in Britain and invented the week-long golf school in America where today 120 pros teach the Jacobs method (almost as well as he does himself).

Even today I seek John out two or three times a year to have a look at my own swing. We may have to negotiate dates because of his passion for trout fishing but he has never let me down. Come to think of it I'd question whether he has ever let anyone down.

Golf has benefitted so much from John's skill as a patient golfing teacher (as long, of course, as you are prepared to listen) and from his shrewd business brain that it is easy to forget he was a Ryder Cup golfer and could play a bit before he turned to full-time teaching.

He has some wonderful stories to tell because he has played with and/or taught the world's greatest names. I know you will enjoy this book as much as he has enjoyed his life in golf. For my part I hope to continue enjoying John Jacobs's company on and off the course for many years to come.

From José Maria Olazabal

John Jacobs is an extraordinary teacher, whose help and advice I have had the benefit of since boyhood. He is both patient and constant, and his influence on my golf and on Spanish golf has been enormous.

From Gary Player

I am very happy to have the opportunity to write an introduction to this book by John Jacobs. Both John and I are actively involved with golf academies, and I know personally the satisfaction derived from transforming a poor player into a fine golfer.

John is a very fine gentleman and an ideal representative of this great game. John was a talented Tour player who always had time for both his fellow competitors and amateur partners. Like myself, John always knew the importance of hard work and was never scared to go that extra mile.

I know you'll enjoy this book and take away many hours of reading pleasure.

From Dave Marr

My first memory of John Jacobs was at the Open Championship of 1970 at St Andrews. As I was hitting balls I became aware that John was scrutinising my swing technique. I knew he had been a player of considerable distinction and I was well aware of his reputation as a teacher. More than that, I knew him to be an evangelist of the game, in the style of Jay Hebert and Jack Burke, a man who was always willing to pass on his specialised knowledge of golf to younger players. He said nothing and I took comfort from his silence. It could mean only one of two things. Either I was totally beyond redemption, and I was confident enough in my ability to dismiss that possibility. Or my game was in good enough shape to leave well alone. I knew he was constitutionally incapable of remaining silent if I had been guilty of some dire sin, so I felt I had passed a test. A little later, when we did talk, I found him to be a pleasant and kindly man. Although there is no great difference in our ages, the word that came to mind was avuncular. I felt him to be someone you could turn to for help in complete confidence if your game went sour.

A decade later we found ourselves as opposing captains of Ryder Cup teams at Walton Heath. My job was to do everything in my power to secure victory, of course, and the problems of my opposite number should have been of no concern to me. But I could not help feeling that John had drawn the short straw that week. For a start, he was denied the services of Seve and, as subsequent events were to prove, that meant he was without Europe's ace in the hole. He led a team of emerging potential, talents in the bud, whereas all my players were in the full flowering of their outstanding powers. I thought then, and still think, that I had the honour to captain the strongest Ryder Cup team ever assembled. I had it easy, John had it tough. He earned my renewed respect for being the fine gentleman he is.

From Mickey Walker

I first met John Jacobs about twenty years ago. At that time John was without doubt the best known golf teacher in Britain and Europe, and every golf magazine had instructional articles written by him.

When I turned professional in 1974 Mark McCormack suggested that I visit John at his Sandown Park Golf Centre. That was when I had the first of many lessons with John, and I continued to visit him for lessons in the USA where he was busy establishing his golf schools.

John not only taught me a lot as a pupil, but I also learned greatly from his teaching methods. Modern technology enables us as teachers to delve into minute details about every aspect of the golf swing, but John's beliefs are still refreshingly simple and easy to understand for beginner and professional alike. 'Two turns and a swish' was, and still is, John's expression of the theory of the golf swing. Simplicity itself, but so true.

Whenever John helped me during my playing career the improvement was immediate. I can recall one particular occasion at Wentworth when after just a few words of advice from John on the practice ground I went on to win a pro-am competition.

I have only in the last few years realised how many golfing careers John has influenced, and what an enormous contribution to golf he has made worldwide. His achievements are endless as a player, teacher, writer, commentator, golf course designer, and executive director of the men's European Tour. I can think of no better host, or better companion. He has been a huge influence on my career, and I feel privileged to know him.

OPENING SHOTS

WALK FIRST, RUN LATER

One of the many attractions of golf is that absolute novices are able, by the happiest of accidents, to hit occasional shots which are absolutely superb. The learner might take a speculative lunge with his four-wood at a ball lying in thick rough and experience that sensuous feeling of purest joy of making solid contact right off the screws. He watches in sheer fascination as the ball soars high and straight, hangs in the air and then begins its descent.

Now comes the moment of exquisite suspense. Will it make the carry over the lake or plummet into the water? Oh rapturous day! There it is, a little bounce on the far bank and bang on line for the flagstick.

His playing partner exclaims: 'Wow! What a shot! Jack Nicklaus himself couldn't have played it better.' He hurries forward in excited anticipation and there, sure enough, the ball has come to rest right by the hole. He is now hooked. From now on it will be golf for the second Jack Nicklaus. By the end of the round scar tissue has already formed over the memory of foozles and bloopers but that four-wood shot is burned deeply into his psyche. That is the image which will sustain him through years of golfing tribulations and keep him coming back for more.

It is an arguable point, and would doubtless be debated with some vehemence by many a neglected golfing wife, but for the sake of discussion we may categorise that wonder shot as a plus, a credit to be entered in black ink in the ledger of life. But that shot also carries a corresponding debit because the experience which turned him into a fanatical golfer is also the factor which prevents him from getting any good at the game.

The reason is that he knows that the combination of his talent and that trusty four-wood is capable of performing wonders and so ever after he has lost no opportunity to attempt another miracle. Despite the accumulating volumes of evidence of disastrous experiences of lost balls, water spouts, breaking glass in the housing estate over the boundary fence on the sixth, sprained wrists and severe censure from exasperated partners, he persists in going for shots which are beyond his capabilities.

In my experience this trait of going for impossible, logic-defying shots far, far beyond the players level or skill and, often enough, anybody else's for that matter, is commonest among highly intelligent men whose success in life has been achieved by the astuteness and practicality of their decisions.

A novice will often ask me to teach him how to play a really advanced recovery shot. He will describe a situation, presumably one which he frequently encounters at his home club, such as a delicate pitch over a hazard to a green sloping downward with the flagstick set close to the edge of the putting surface. 'How do you play those little cut-ups out of the long grass that pitch just over the brow of the green, and take a couple of hops, and then spin back to the flag?'

On these occasions I am reminded of the girl carrying the violin case who asked a New York cabbie how to get to Carnegie Hall and he replied: 'Lots of practice, lady.' I suppose the golfing equivalent would be to tell the pupil to become good enough to turn pro, then win ten major championships over

4

a twenty-year career and then go out and buy a rabbit's foot.

Every great player's game is based on a thorough appreciation of his limitations. He plays to his strengths, which is another way of saying the same thing. How odd, then, that bad golfers are so convinced that they have no limitations. The golfer who always plays the shot he knows for certain he can pull off may not get a reputation as a big hitter or a virtuoso stroke maker but he will win an awful lot of bets.

BRING YOUR MIND
INTO PLAY

I played in four Open Championships at St Andrews and never, as I felt, did myself justice. I actually had a chance of winning, in 1955, until both my playing companion, Christy O'Connor, and I took sevens at the fourteenth. To score well on the Old Course you have to make hay on the loop, that runs at the end of the course, of two par-threes and two very short par-fours.

I could never get my due ration of threes on the loop and the ninth hole in particular gave me problems. I always seemed to hit my pitch twenty yards short of the flag or thirty yards beyond it. The difficulty of this hole is that it has no difficulties on it. It is flat and completely unblemished by bunkers or trees or bushes or burns, nothing at all to assist your depth perception.

Yardage charts are virtually useless on the British

championship links because of the customary turbulent air conditions, with or without rain, hail or snow. The golfer has to rely on his instincts and his senses of sight and feel and they need visual evidence in order to provide useful feedback. On that ninth hole there is only an expanse of nothingness.

My eventual solution was to create an imaginary bunker and visualise it sitting in front of the green. Now my mind's eye had something to work on. The ball had to fly that obstacle and now my subconscious could factor in the wind strength and direction, and the lie of the ball, and when the wheels stopped whirring round I had my print-out: 'Go with a crisp nine-iron over the left edge of that imaginary hazard with a touch of fade.'

If you think all this is rather far-fetched, or even grounds for calling the men in white coats to incarcerate the madman who actually invents extra bunkers for a course which is already pock-marked with craters like the battlefield of the Somme, I must tell you that all good golfers play similar mind games. When playing downwind Lee Trevino visualises a large tree dead ahead. Having to clear that tree makes him get the ball up and flying and therefore obtaining maximum benefit from wind assistance.

How often have you seen a pro on the tee of a short hole hold his hands alongside his head like blinkers? He is eliminating the wing bunkers from his vision, and from his imagination, and getting a positive picture of his task. A very common trick for removing the threat of intervening water is to stare at the lake and visualise it freezing over. Hold that picture in the mind and you play the shot without a care in the world.

While the golfer can play tricks with his mind, this is a two-way process and the mind can equally play tricks with the golfer. At one stage in his career whenever Max Faulkner surveyed a putt he was horrified to see the hole filling up with cement and he had to take a hurried stab to get the ball up to the hole while there was still a hole for it to fall into. When that happens it is time to leave the clubs in the cupboard for a bit.

PRIORITIES OF GOLF

Teachers are sometimes accused of being obsessed by technique, believing this to be the be-all and end-all of golf, and ignoring the equally important mental side of the game. In entering a plea of Not Guilty to this accusation I would make one amendment to the wording of the charge. The mental side, in my opinion, is not equally important as technique; it is the most important element in golf. My priorities are: 1. temperament 2. technique 3. physical strength. The golfer who completely confirmed me in my opinion was Gary Player. As a young man when he first visited Britain he had a terrible swing. I remember the late and much-lamented Leonard Crawley, a fine amateur and a good judge of the golf swing, remarking that Gary would never do any good in the game. I demurred because Gary had about him an inner fire and a lust for success that simply could not be denied. He worked at his game like a man possessed. And he sought advice from anyone and everyone he thought might help, always in the politest and most respectful of terms.

'Excuse me, Mr Jacobs, but would you mind if I asked you a question about the grip?' His very appearance, with those piercing eyes of a bird of prey, marked him out as a man of destiny. So I pointed out to Leonard that

Gary had the character to make his horrible swing work, and repeat consistently, and win. After all, anyone can improve his technique but he is lumbered for life with the temperament with which he was born. And in this context Gary was a born champion.

We practised a lot together and, like everyone else he approached, I helped him as much as I could. His swing improved and was good enough to dismiss me from a match play tournament in the first round. The next winter I went to play in South Africa and my game went to pot. Gary was most solicitous and helped me back into the groove, to such effect that I beat him in the final of the South African Match Play Championship. Talk about role reversal! But that little story illustrates the camaraderie which for me is the very soul of professional golf.

Gary went from success to success and became one of the Big Three. In the company of Arnold Palmer and Jack Nicklaus the diminutive Player was seriously out-gunned. He determined to build up his physique and strength to the point where he could hold his own against the longest hitters in the game. He went into serious, not to say punishing, training and thereby got into the habit of daily physical exercising, a habit which has kept him competitive on the Senior Tour at an age when most athletes are running only to fat.

HAVEN'T WE MET BEFORE

Sean Connery is a fanatical golfer and he used to come to me for lessons at my Sandown Park Golf Centre at Esher. On one occasion he rang me and asked if I would help him with his game that evening because he had an important golfing date. I explained that I was fully engaged because that was the evening I set aside for walking up and down the practice bays having a word or two with each of the clients. I have developed a facility for spotting the destructive fault at a glance and can therefore get a pupil to hit the ball solidly with a simple word or two of advice. You can imagine the word-of-mouth publicity value of this evening of free golfing tips.

So I told Sean that if he would like to come to the centre and get into a bay near the start of the line I would certainly cast an eye over his swing and put him on the right track. This I did and he then suggested we have supper together when I knocked off about nine o'clock. That was agreed and I continued my duties as golfing evangelist putting the clients on to the path of righteousness.

The common emotional state of people at driving ranges fluctuates between frustration and despair and they are usually pathetically grateful when a word in season gets them hitting the ball off the middle of the club-face and, above all, soaring into the night sky rather than scuttling along the turf.

The incident did at least have the virtue of novelty when I stopped to watch one attractive woman's labours and asked if I might make so bold as to offer a word of advice, only to be told: 'Leave me alone, I'm doing perfectly well on my own.'

I proceeded on my way and duly presented myself for supper at nine o'clock. You can surely guess who (the then) Mrs Sean Connery turned out to be: the actress Diane Cilento, no golfing novice, who had spurned my offer of help. We made our peace over a very decent bottle of claret.

A YOUNG PRODIGY

I have been teaching for the Spanish Golf Federation for twenty-five years. On my visits I teach the pros how to teach in the mornings and in the afternoons I coach the junior squads, the cream of young Spanish golfers.

I was thrilled by the prospects of a thirteen-year-old called José Maria Olazabal when I first saw him. He was a very good hitter but what impressed me most was his character. They say that sculptors can see the statue within the rock. If ever I saw a champion within the boy it was José Maria, or Chema as his friends call him. Of course, he quickly endorsed my judgment by winning the Boys', Youths' and Amateur Championships, the only player ever to capture all three of the premier British amateur titles at every age level.

At the 1993 Ryder Cup match at The Belfry, Chema was obviously off form. I went to the European captain,

Bernard Gallacher, an old friend and former pupil, and offered my help, if Chema would like it. He was only too glad of the offer and we went to work on the practice ground. He had fallen into the habit of straightening his right leg on the backswing and he had the ball too far back in his stance. As a result he was turning his six-iron into a five-iron and hitting push-hooks.

I restored some flex into his knees and sorted out the ball position and generally got him back to where he should be. These remedial adjustments are not instant cures as a rule. The player has to persevere and work on them for weeks, months, even years sometimes before they fully exorcise the demons of faulty style and become second nature.

Some golfers want their teacher at hand at every tournament to monitor progress and supervise the golfing equivalent of physiotherapy. I find this absolutely incomprehensible and possibly detrimental since so much attention could create too much detailed information and produce what is often called paralysis through analysis. For my own part I would not dream of traipsing all round the world in the tow of a neurotic golfer.

Fortunately, Chema does not require a physician dancing attendance on him as a permanent member of his retinue. He told me some time after our session at the Ryder Cup: 'I know what you mean. I am working at it and I am getting better.'

He most certainly was, as he demonstrated by winning the Masters and the World Series in 1994. Results like that are satisfaction enough for a teacher but Chema elevated himself even higher in my estimation by making generous public acknowledgment of my help. And that is something which does not happen with every great player. Not by a long way.

NOT MUCH CHOICE

To meet the charming, relaxed and softly spoken Tommy Bolt away from the golf course you could hardly credit that this was the same man with the shortest of fuses to the most violent temper in the game. He would curse and swear and throw more clubs in one round than most golfers would get through in a lifetime. It is an old story and I make no apologies for repeating it but it is one of my favourites and perhaps there is someone out there who has not heard the quintessential Tommy Bolt anecdote. Late in his career he came to the last hole with a chance to win and meticulously paced out the 166 yards of his shot to the green.

'What do you think?' he asked his caddie.

'Well, boss, it's either a two-iron or a nine-iron.'

'Come on,' said Bolt, 'I was thinking of maybe a six-iron.'

'No sir,' said the caddie. 'It's gotta be the two-iron or the nine-iron 'cos they's the only ones we got left.'

WATERY COINCIDENCE

In the final round of the Centenary Open in 1960 I was on the first green of the Old Course at St Andrews when there was a sudden deluge of rain, so intense that within a second or so the green was a moving sheet of water and my ball was being borne inexorably towards the Swilcan burn. I was ready with my marker and the moment my ball came to a temporary halt I marked it and saved it and myself from a cruel and undeserved fate.

At that moment the chairman of the Championship Committee, Tom Harvey, came up and told us to mark our balls and discontinue play. That round was subsequently cancelled and Kel Nagle had to wait another day before becoming, as his myriad friends would surely insist, one of the nicest men ever to win the championship.

At the following year's championship, at Royal Birkdale, I was on the first green during the third round when a tremendous storm broke. In moments we were surrounded by water. I sent for a ruling and who should come up but Tom Harvey. Once again he told us to mark our balls and discontinue play. And again the round had to be cancelled and play resumed the next day.

Some time later we both had to speak at a dinner at the House of Commons and Tom Harvey warned the company of the danger they were incurring by bringing the two of us together, before allaying any wild speculation about a dangerous blood feud by telling the story of our two previous meetings.

THE VIDEO NASTY

Teaching standards have risen appreciably in recent years and sophisticated techniques such as video play-backs can be very valuable aids in pointing out a swing fault and how it affects the shot.

But for me video has one serious limitation: it does not show the club-face at impact. It cannot be stressed too often or too strongly that delivering the club-face square to the ball is absolutely the Number One priority in the golf swing. Without it, everything else is meaningless.

If you video your swing and play it back to a teacher he might very well say: 'I can see nothing wrong there; you have a very good swing'. But if you make that very good swing with the driver and the club-face is open or closed by four degrees then the ball will head for the woods every time.

It is a pernicious fault because more often than not the player will try to adjust his swing to accommodate his errant club-face. You see dozens of them every time you look along the practice range, open-faced golfers trying to hit the fairway by aiming left. The only result they achieve from their practice sessions is to make a bad fault worse, grooving a destructive action.

If I were to approach one of those golfers I can pretty well guarantee that when I make some adjustments he will then hit shots which give him a vision of how well he *could* play. It does not follow by any means that the transformation will be permanent. Under the pressures

14

of real golf out on the course players tend to revert to their habitual faults.

And then they go around saying that John Jacobs's lessons are like Chinese meals, two hours later you are slicing again. That is a cross that teachers have to bear. Any swing adjustment needs work and practice and perseverance if a permanent cure is to be achieved.

With tongue in cheek I often tell pupils: 'What a good job you can't keep what I have just given you. I would never see you again.' I say this, of course, only to those with a sense of humour. Anyone who plays this great game has to have a sense of humour.

GIVE IT YOUR ALL

I am not one of those teachers who advocate that a golfer should play within himself using, say, only eighty per cent power, as if anyone of us is capable of making such a measurement. I believe it is easier to hit the ball with as much power as you can muster without losing your balance.

By the same token, when you are between clubs I would normally go for the weaker club and make a full-blooded hit. If you select the club which is strong for the distance it is vital to grip down the shaft and give the shot the full treatment. Soft or quiet shots using a portion of your power are much more difficult.

When Severiano Ballesteros blew his chances in the Masters with that infamous second shot into the pond on Augusta's fifteenth hole in 1986 it was clear the moment he made contact that the club-head was decelerating in the hitting area. Subconsciously he knew that the club in his hands was too strong for the distance. In Seve's defence he was having to wait and watch Jack Nicklaus going mad in front of him.

By contrast, when José Maria Olazabal was in a similar position on that hole in the 1994 Masters he selected a club which needed to be hit a hundred per cent perfectly and with all his power in order to carry to the green.

Of course, this doctrine requires that the player has a realistic idea of how far he hits each club. Regrettably most handicap golfers kid themselves about their power.

PHYSICIAN HEAL THYSELF? NOT AT MY AGE!

When I retired from competitive golf I lost enthusiasm for my own game and hardly played for many years. I had a living to make and in this I was greatly helped by a man who was to become one of the great influences in my life. Laddie Lucas, the left-handed Walker Cup player, was a member at my club, Sandy Lodge in Hertfordshire, and also, of course, a much-decorated fighter ace from the war. I had also served in the RAF so we had two strong interests in common, but it was the fact that we got on so well on a personal level that led us into a business partnership.

From that sprang the pioneering idea of formally structured golf centres and the ones we built in Britain and Ireland remain the models for golf centres and schools all over the world. Add writing books and magazine articles, coaching the national teams of ten countries, doing television commentaries, making films and videos, giving private lessons around the world, group instruction, setting up the PGA European Tour and teaching the teachers for the John Jacobs Golf Centres in America – all intensely golf-related activities – and you can see how I became over-golfed without even playing the game.

For relaxation I preferred fly fishing. But in the last five years or so, as I eased off on my working schedule, I have rediscovered the joys of playing the game. I must confess that in my capacity as a professional golf analyst I cannot give myself high marks for style or performance these days. I experiment and do things I tell others not to do. But I do enjoy it, and that, after all, is the purpose of golf.

GIVE OR THROW YOUR DRIVER AWAY

Naturally enough many of my pupils are long-handicap players, often well stricken in years. A good proportion of them complain that they cannot use their drivers:

'I've got a good enough swing with the four-wood but my driver swing can't seem to get the ball airborne.'

In fact the pupil's swing is exactly the same with both clubs although the results are dramatically different. People do not appreciate how the loft on a golf club forgives faults in technique, the more loft the more forgiving. Try it. Go out and deliberately try to slice a ball with your wedge.

So when a long handicapper of a certain age complains that he can't use his driver I give him the most helpful piece of advice he will ever receive: 'If I were you, I would give your driver to your worst enemy.'

ARMS OR BODY?

Historically there have been two fundamentally opposed views of the golf swing.

One lot, with the great teacher Ernest Jones leading the way, saw the golf swing as mainly a product of hand and arm action. The other and even greater Jones, Bobby of that ilk, endorsed this doctrine and was the supreme exemplar of a style which calls for no input from leg or upper-body action other than to move out of the way of the swinging club, or 'clearing the hips' in instructional jargon. To some people that expression smacks of serfs being swept aside into the gutter to allow free passage for some mighty nabob.

The immortal Sam Snead was an exponent of the Jones method as were two of the finest women golfers of all time, Babe Zaharias, who was one of Ernest Jones's pupils, and Joyce Wethered, whose swing was described by Bobby Jones as the best he had ever seen. Add Gene Littler, Christy O'Connor and a few others and you could assemble a formidable team to represent the school of sweet swingers. I might add that I would be cheering for this team from the sidelines, but for sentimental reasons rather than conviction.

During the First World War my father served in a Sportsman's Battalion with Ernest Jones on the Western Front and had the grim task of carrying his friend out of the trenches near Loos in 1915 when a German shell smashed Ernie's leg so badly that the remains had to be amputated. It says a lot for Jones's ideas about the golf swing that he recovered to play just as well on one leg as he had on two, scoring seventy-two in the second round he played, while walking between shots on crutches.

The other school of thought – we may call them the Hitters as opposed to the Swingers – was inspired by Ben Hogan and reproduces the action of a boxer throwing a punch, digging his spikes into the turf, kicking into the shot with the right leg and making the rotation of his body the main source of pulling power along a straight left arm. Some people talk of 'leverage' in this action but that is a misnomer. If we care to line up a Hitters team under the captaincy of Ben Hogan we might nominate Arnold Palmer, Jack Nicklaus, Gary Player and Raymond Floyd for starters.

Do not ask me to prophesy the winners of our match of the styles. Most golf competitions are not won with strokes of exceptional power or virtuosity; they are won around and, even more particularly, on the greens where touch and feel supersede all questions of swing versus hit. That does not mean that my position on the subject is firmly on the fence.

I reject the concept of two styles in competition with each other, with the implication that one of them must be the better of the two. I also reject the idea of teaching 'a method', whether it be the Ernest Jones method, the Ben Hogan method, the David Leadbetter method or even the John Jacobs method.

There has never been a John Jacobs method and never will be. I do not even teach people, as my approach is sometimes described. I teach one individual, the person who is with me at the time. I assess that person's physical capabilities and potential, diagnose his or her faults and prescribe the remedy suitable for that individual.

It could be that in the course of a day I am consulted by three golfers all suffering from the same problem, say slicing. I might well give them three completely different remedies because in golf, as in medicine, the treatment must be suited to the individual patient. I even feel slightly uneasy addressing the world in a book. My instinct is to place large placards in every book shop reading: 'Instead of buying this book, write to me describing your golfing problems and I will write you an individual letter with my suggestions to cure your maladies.' But please don't. I have little enough time for my favourite pursuits with rod and gun as it is.

GOLF WITH THE NERVE REMOVED

Hitting a few balls into a net may be all very well to loosen up before you play but extended practice sessions in a net can be dangerous. I had a low-handicap friend who went skiing in Switzerland every winter and in order to keep his golf swing in trim he went to one of the golf schools in Cran-sur-Sierre in the evenings and hit buckets of balls into a net. When he returned to our Sandy Lodge club he had the biggest hook you ever saw.

In a net you have none of the fears you encounter on the course, such as woods and rough and ponds and out-of-bounds. So you swing easily and the tendency is to hit harder and harder and sometimes for the grip to get stronger and stronger. You need to see the flight of the ball when you practise so that you can detect a fault and remedy it before it develops into a full-blown habit.

WHEN THE WIND BLOWS

Because golf is a side-on game and the club-head swings through the ball in an in-to-in arc, the standard shot is a slight draw. So if your ball flies just perceptibly from right to left in flight do not try to correct your 'fault'; it is quite normal.

Because of this tendency to a slight draw it is unwise to practise in a left-to-right wind. I want the beginner to have that picture of the ball easing to the left so I don't want a left-to-right wind destroying it. A right-to-left wind helps that image and the golfer learns to swing in sympathy with it. I would always suggest finding a place to practise against the wind or with it slightly right-to-left.

Playing into the wind calls for the club-face to be

'strong' at address, with the right shoulder high, a shorter backswing and a good unwind of the body through the ball. Downwind the club-face should be 'weak' at address, with the left shoulder high. The swing should be long and you should feel to be hitting up and under. It is not advisable to practise downwind; there is a tendency to hang back on the right foot and hit too early so practising downwind may induce faults rather than virtues.

A TELLING COMBINATION

There is a perverse streak in golfers. Possibly it runs right throughout human nature, but this streak is most easily identified in golfers, since the game has a powerful tendency to strip us of the protective camouflage of our souls.

The streak in question is an insistent siren voice from within which whispers: 'Yes, yes, that's all very well but I am an exception to that rule.' The rules in question may range from an exhortation to grip the club lightly to the law which insists that you must not drive home from the club after two strong belts of the hard stuff.

In one respect my streak is doubly perverse because I tell myself 'Yes, yes, that's all very well but I am an exception to that rule' in regard to my own rule that men should never on any account teach their wives to drive a car or play golf.

In the early fifties when I was the newly married

professional at Sandy Lodge Golf Club my wife Rita partnered me in the club's very popular mixed foursomes competitions. She has never been a really serious golfer, which is just as well since I have quite enough fanaticism for the two of us, but for a twenty-four handicapper she had elements in her game which could be exploited to make her a very useful mixed foursomes partner. She was very straight off the tee with her three-wood, and through the green her little five-wood could be relied upon to keep the ball in play.

She was not interested in taking formal instruction but one day, on the eve of a mixed foursomes competition, she asked if she could come over to the practice range for a quick lesson. In defiance of my own rule, I replied: 'Of course, darling.'

I started into my usual routine of Diagnosis, Explanation and Correction when she stopped me in my tracks: 'Don't tell me all about it; just give me one thing to think about tomorrow.'

I must stress that what I told her should not be taken as one of the Ten Commandments for a good swing. She had a personal idiosyncrasy in her action which needed a slighty unconventional remedy. Her natural tendency was to turn her shoulders from the top which meant that her arms and hands and, indeed, the golf club were largely passive in the downswing. I told her to start the downswing by casting the club-head with hands and arms.

The result was astonishing. At the first hole, a par-five, I drove, she hit her five-wood and I knocked the ball on to the green. At the next, a par-four, she played her three-wood off the tee and I hit my three-wood on to the green. At the par-three third I hit the green and we two-putted. And so it went on. Rita was still no better than a twenty-four handicapper but by playing to her strengths we melded into such a formidable partnership that the club, wrongly thinking that I was the strength of the partnership, eventually had *me* playing off plus-eight!

I didn't mind. After all, it would never do for the professional to win club competitions. That was not club policy, of course. The club would not have minded a bit if Rita and I had been winners. That was my own rule and one to which I would never say: 'Yes, yes, that's all very well but I am an exception to that rule.'

HIT FOR SIX

Practice rounds can be terribly slow, and none slower than the occasion when I was playing with Peter Alliss at St Andrews. We hit putt after putt on the fifth green while waiting for the sixth fairway to clear until at last I was able to call to him from the side of the green that it was time to move on. He picked up my ball and bowled it to me overarm. Responding to this cricketing motif I swung my putter and by the most amazing fluke caught the ball absolutely flush. The ball flew like a bullet and almost decapitated someone on the twelfth green.

Having established that nobody had in fact been injured we played on but when we finished I was given the dread news that the R & A secretary required my presence in his office. Forthwith. The formidable Brigadier Brickman duly gave me a thorough and well-deserved dressing down. I expressed my sincere regrets and that was that.

He was a man of great charm and, having done his duty, he switched the conversation to more congenial topics. We soon discovered a mutual and abiding interest in fishing and cricket and so began a firm friendship which strengthened and endured until the day he died.

THE DOGGY VICTIMS OF INEXORABLE FATE

It was never my life's ambition to teach golf. In the 1950s I wanted to be a great champion and to that end I had to keep myself fit and strong and healthy, jogging daily with my Irish Setter, Skittles. At the age of 39 I took stock of my situation and faced up to the increasingly obvious fact that I was not going to make it to the very highest level of the game.

By coincidence Skittles chose that moment to make it obvious that arthritic joints had stifled all enthusiasm for the daily exercise. So we both quit. I went into the business of teaching golf and lost all interest in playing the game. For the next twenty-five years I hardly played at all.

Now, in semi-retirement, I have rediscovered the joy of playing, notwithstanding the diminished powers which inevitably attend the ageing process. But my return to golf has meant a like return to a fitness regime and not a day goes by without a long walk through the New Forest with Polly, the latest in a long sequence of black Labradors.

FADE VERSUS SLICE

Most people have the idea that a fade is simply a less virulent slice and that the only practical difference is that a fade slides away to the right side of the fairway while a slice sails deep into the woods. Let me give you a graphic example of the real difference between these two left-to-right shots.

One of my members at Sandy Lodge was an elderly gentleman whose favourite club was a baffy, or, for the benefit of younger readers, the equivalent of a five-wood. He hit across the ball from out-to-in with an open face and brought the club-head *steeply downwards into the ball at an angle, as I should judge, of at least thirty degrees.*

It was with this club and this method that he had a hole in one at the 105 yard eighth hole one day when we were playing together. He gave that shot the full treatment, so we can see that the main characteristic of the slice is loss of length; the side spin is a subsidiary symptom. The fade, on the other hand, is caused by the club-head approaching the ball on a shallow arc but making contact with the club-face open, hence imparting side spin. The ball still goes a long way but the shot can be very inaccurate, depending on the swing direction.

A swing from the inside with the face open on a shallow arc sends the ball a long way to the right. A swing from the outside with the face open on a shallow

arc can be both long and straight, as in the case of Lee
Trevino.

TEACHER BEWARE

Almost immediately after being demobilised from the
RAF I was out on the practice tee giving lessons. Bomber
squadron flight engineers get very few opportunities for
golf in wartime, as might well be imagined, and my game
was rusty. In case any of my pupils from that period
should read this, let me hasten to add that no claims
for rebates can be entertained after so long an interval,
but I realised later that I was relating my teaching to
the problems I was having with my own golf. This must
always be a danger, since our own troubles inevitably
flavour our ideas.

I always stress to trainee teachers for the John Jacobs
Centres that they must focus tightly on the individual
pupil and try to get inside his or her mind. After all, if
the instructor can feel what the pupil feels, and suffer
what the pupil suffers, and understand what the pupil
understands, then it will be much easier for him to
provide enlightenment. Imparting that enlightenment
must be a strictly disciplined progression. First the
teacher asks the pupil to hit a ball and he watches
the flight of the shot. The way the ball behaves tells him
precisely what the club-face is doing at impact. He can
now explain the whys and wherefores of the club-face
deviations in precise detail.

I believe it is most important to ensure that the pupil

truly understands this explanation. Just telling a pupil to move his right hand slightly more on top of the shaft may be correct advice to cure his fault but that advice will carry much more weight if the pupil understands and appreciates the specific reasons for this adjustment, and how it will change the presentation of the club-face to the ball.

A very common reaction on such occasions is the complaint that the change feels uncomfortable. My response is that a change is bound to feel a little uncomfortable at first, but persevere and it will become second nature. Some pupils persevere only in repeating the complaint that it feels uncomfortable. In these cases it is easy enough to recognise the common blockage in the pupil–teacher relationship: he-doesn't-know-how-I-feel-and-I-know-damn-well-that-I-will-play-better-gripping-the-club-my-way.

If the pupil persists in complaining that it feels uncomfortable there is only one response: 'Well, get comfortable then – and go on slicing.' Nearly always, however, that attitude can be broken down by making sure the pupil understands in specific detail why a change has to be made.

SLIGHTLY STRETCHED

Many people have speculated on the reason why so many professional golfers are avid fishermen. The commonest theory is that fishing makes the perfect antidote to the stresses of concentrating like mad for five or more hours a day on the golf course, because a man can unwind and relax both his mind and his body on the riverbank. That explanation tells us just one thing: that the writer knows nothing about fishing.

One affinity between the two sports is that both require intense concentration. The man who slumps somnolently in a deckchair with a line and float on the water, trusting that the little bell will awake him from his slumbers when a fish takes the hook, is not a fisherman: he is a man who uses fishing as an excuse for doing nothing.

Most of the golfing fishermen I know, including Jack Nicklaus, Tom Weiskopf and Nick Faldo, take the sport very seriously indeed, as I do. My only regret is that fishing cannot emulate golf and provide a handicapping system. You can't catch half a fish. When I say that both golf and fishing must be taken seriously I do not mean solemnly, although I could have done with a touch of solemnity on the day I went coarse fishing with Lionel Platts, a Ryder Cup team-mate, and David Snell, who was assistant to my cousin Jack at Lindrick.

There was a terrific wind blowing and as we were loading our tackle into the boat it slipped its moorings and started to drift away. I grabbed it by the gunnel but could not restrain it and my companions had to grab me by the ankles as I was being stretched like a human hawser between boat and jetty, yelling and spluttering as my face was immersed in the water. The other two were laughing so hard that they could hardly keep grip of my ankles.

As I was saying, it is extremely important for fishermen to concentrate on what they are doing.

TALKING OF THE UNMENTIONABLE

The majority of shanks are caused by the player standing with his shoulders wide open. This 'outside' stance creates a flat backswing whereby the backswing ends with the club travelling backwards instead of upwards. The downswing becomes forwards instead of downwards, hence the shank. In any backswing there is some inside element and some upward.

My remedy is to address the ball with the shoulders closed, giving the feeling that the swing is going to be inside and leaving the mind free to swing the club up on the inside, from where it will come down.

A shank is often a classic example of a little knowledge being dangerous. An open stance is desirable, i.e. feet open but shoulders square. An across stance, with the shoulders open, is used when we wish to swing out-to-in, as for bunker shots.

HOLES IN ONE

I had a very good friend who was Commander-in-Chief of the Pakistan Air Force. He used to visit us at Sandy Lodge when he came to Britain and I would give him lessons. He invited me to visit Pakistan to teach golf to his air force and as a special reward he took me in a helicopter up into the mountains to fish streams where men had never fished before, a truly magical experience. My friend was subsequently made Minister of Tourism and he commissioned me to design several golf courses in Pakistan.

On a subsequent visit I was playing at Peshawar and when I reached the tee of the short twelfth hole my friend, who was playing an adjacent hole, called across to say that his companion, the local pro, had just had a hole in one at the seventeenth. 'Oh yes,' I replied in a casual tone, 'just watch and I'll show you how it's done.' So saying I took my three-iron and, to my well-concealed amazement, hit the ball straight into the hole.

With golf being in its infancy in Pakistan the word immediately spread that I could make a hole in one at will! A helicopter was produced and I was commanded to fly down to Lahore so that the President of Pakistan, Ayub Khan, could meet this foreign wizard. In fact, the President was having his own piece of fun at my expense. He was a very experienced golfer and knew perfectly well that nobody could produce a hole in one to order. But we spent a very enjoyable evening together talking golf.

Two other holes in one were rather special for me. One winter's day I went for a day's golf at Sunningdale with the Hunt brothers, Bernard and Geoffrey, both Ryder Cup players. I had an assistant from the pro's shop as a partner and managed, not without considerable persuasion, to get Bernard Hunt to agree to a wager of £5 on the round. We played the New Course and the Hunts won three and two. On the tee of the par-three seventeenth I proposed that we play the bye for double or quits. Bernard said: 'With a name and a nose like yours you'll probably get a hole in one.' And so I did.

The third occasion was the least likely ace of them all. Frank Pennink, the golf course architect who also wrote magazine articles on golf, was a very gifted amateur. He thought it would be an enjoyable and instructive exercise if he played a round of golf with all the members of the 1955 Ryder Cup team and described their special qualities.

By the time he came to Sandy Lodge to play me he had done all the others and was at a loss as to what to say about my game. He had already written about Harry Weetman's prodigious long hitting, and Ken Bousfield's magical short game and Dai Rees's straightness and had pretty well covered every aspect of the game. It happened to be blowing a tremendous gale that day and in jocular vein I said that I would demonstrate precise control of the ball in fierce conditions. Then I only went and holed out with a two-iron on the short fifteenth!

A DISCREET SILENCE

On the eve of the final against Gary Player in the South African Match Play Championship we received word that my wife's father had died. Rita took the next morning's flight back to London. She was sitting next to three air crew of South African Airways and as the plane approached Nairobi one of them went forward to the flight deck and returned with the dire news: 'That roineck is one up on Gary!' Rita said not a word.

At Athens another enquiry was made of the radio reports and back came the stupefying news: 'That roineck has beaten Gary on the last green!'

Only now did their travelling companion permit herself the immense pleasure of announcing: 'I am Mrs John Jacobs, the wife of that roineck.'

LEGS WERE MADE FOR WALKING

I was naturally apprehensive when I opened my first golf school in America, near Scottsdale, Arizona. This was the first such establishment in the United States so my initial class of senior citizens, average age of sixty or so, did not know what to expect of the school, nor did they know anything about the Englishman who was to instruct them. Enlightenment on both counts was offered at a welcoming cocktail party.

One man said to me: 'I am hoping you will give me a grooved swing.'

'I'm sure you've brought one of those with you,' I replied. 'My task will most likely be to give you a different one.'

They were to report to the teaching area at eight a.m. When I arrived they were all hitting balls. The common denominator in what might loosely be termed their swings was a curling-under action on the backswing, followed by a lunge into the shot with a drive of the legs. Balls were flying all over the place. Drastic action was clearly needed before my class suffered self-inflicted wounds and mental trauma.

'In Britain we have been playing golf for three hundred years,' I told them. 'Over here you have been playing golf for a hundred years. Isn't it curious, then, that it is only recently that we have discovered the paramount importance of the legs in the golf swing?'

So saying, I teed up a ball, stood on one leg and hit a drive, a very good one as it happened. My party trick was greeted by a mystified silence. I hit three more one-legged drives. They got the message.

Now that I had established a receptive mood, I instructed them to turn on the backswing until they felt that the club was pointing in the direction of the target and then swing the club-head through the ball. Suddenly, and for the first time for most of them, they started making solid contact at impact and the ball flew not only in roughly the required direction but for satisfying distances. Both pupils and teacher had safely hurdled the first barrier.

LET THE WIND
BE YOUR ALLY

I love playing golf in a wind, just so long as it is not so strong as to blow you off balance. The basic rule of windy golf is this: with the distance clubs (i.e. the driver) you aim off and allow the wind to bring the ball back on to your target; with shots to the green you make suitable adjustments and fight the wind.

WIND AGAINST: you want a shallow arc to give the ball a penetrating flight. At the address de-loft the face of the club by raising the right shoulder slightly and take a shorter backswing. Sweep the club-head through the ball as you turn through. Try to leave the peg standing.

DOWNWIND: increase the loft of the club by raising the left shoulder at the address. Make a long, full up-and-under swing.

LEFT-TO-RIGHT: off the tee – aim left with the driver and give the shot plenty of height; or aim straight, take your three-wood and close the face. With lofted irons – underclub. If the shot calls for a five-iron take your six-iron, aim straight at the target and hit the ball really hard. Hitting extra hard induces a slight hook which will keep your ball on target.

RIGHT-TO-LEFT: off the tee – whack your driver down

the right-hand side of the fairway. With irons – you can't float the shot on the wind into the green from the right because the ball will pitch and run off the back left of the green. Therefore open the face and cut the ball into the wind. This will necessitate taking a stronger club, depending on the strength of the wind, maybe a five-iron for a seven-iron distance.

A TIMELY UPPERCUT
FOR THE CHAMPION

At the 1969 Open Championship at Royal Lytham I went out to watch Jack Nicklaus play a practice round with Gary Player and Gardner Dickinson. As he stood to the ball, the back of Nicklaus's neck was absolutely parallel to the ground and this was making him rock back away from the ball and then tilt under on the downswing. The ball was going all over the place.

This travesty continued until the sixth tee when Jack turned to me and said: 'You're supposed to know something about this game. What do you think?'

I answered: 'Doesn't anyone ever talk posture to you?'

'It's funny you should say that,' he said. 'Jack Grout [his first and only teacher] sometimes feints to put an uppercut under my chin.'

'You should take a lesson from Mr Grout,' I advised.

Since Jack Grout was back home in Ohio, I was commanded to substitute for him. I gave my standard remedial treatment for the dreaded tilt while the traffic backed up behind us. Needless to say, I got the blame for holding up the play. As with most engrained faults, Jack's tilt was not eliminated at a stroke. He still has to fight a tendency to rock the shoulders rather than turn them.

The destructive effect of tilting was never more dramatically demonstrated than in the case of my great friend Harold Henning who retired prematurely from competitive golf and returned home to South Africa. I didn't see him for five years and then I received a telephone call from Pat, his wife, saying: 'Harold does nothing but play bridge and if he doesn't get back into golf I shall divorce him. You've got to help.' Together we managed to get his game back into good enough shape for him to enjoy a second successful career on the US Senior Tour.

NEVER UP, NEVER WIN

How often have you had the experience of everything resting on the last putt of the match and watching your partner belt the putt so hard that the ball races past or even clear over the top of the hole? He then turns with a soppy expression of contrition on his face and tries to excuse his imbecility by saying: 'Well, I had to give it a chance.'

That is exactly what he did not do. The ball had no chance of dropping at that speed. That hoary old expression 'never up, never in' is frequently trotted out on these occasions, adding banality to injury.

Some, like Gary Player, have the courage to rap short putts so firmly that they can be hit straight into the hole, ignoring any breaks. Most of the great putters, including Bobby Jones and Bobby Locke, played their putts with just enough speed to die into the hole. This policy makes the hole much wider on short putts. On long putts, most good players concentrate on distance above all and try to get the exact speed to carry the ball up to the hole and no farther. If the ball should drop then that is a bonus but it is not the original intention. The control of speed, or weight, is the vital factor in judging the amount of break the ball will take. On the longer putts distance is more important than direction.

SLICES OF WISDOM
AND IGNORANCE

In 1978 I was teaching a group of businessmen in the USA and we suspended our activities to watch the closing sequence of the Masters tournament. No sooner had we switched on the TV than a commentator remarked: 'He came over that one' in response to Gary Player having hit a shot left of target.

That expression about coming over the ball, meaning bringing the club-head into the ball on an out-to-in path, is a favourite of TV pundits to explain pulls and hooks but it is by no means apposite in every case, and well wide of the mark in describing Player's shot.

Gary is not given to understatement and when he goes

through a patch of what he describes as 'martyrdom to the worst hook you ever saw' he is certainly not coming over the shot, quite the reverse. In short, he is coming too much under the ball on an in-to-out path which causes the wrists to roll over, closing the club-face.

I explained this to the assembled company and shortly after the end of play the local pro entered the room and said: 'Did you see that? Gary Player came over every shot!' He was surprised that his remark got a good laugh.

'Yes. He came over the ball sixty-four times and won the Masters,' I said.

If the causes of pulls and hooks are sometimes misdiagnosed then the same is true, only more so, in the case of slicing. The slice is the commonest fault, virtually a universal disease. Sometimes if a new pupil is a pretty girl and I happen to be in roguish mood I will open the proceedings by looking into her eyes and saying: 'I bet you slice with the driver and the long irons, pull your short irons and hit pretty straight with the four-wood and the six-iron.'

The look of awe and astonishment which greets this magical utterance is better than a whole bottle of rejuvenation pills. 'How on earth . . . ?'

I do not explain that the law of probabilities made my guess a near-certainty. I have the pupil's rapt attention and she will treat my every word as holy writ. That makes teaching easy and effective.

It may sound incongruous that this same standard should hit the ball left with the short irons and right with the longer clubs. That apparent anomaly is explained by the loft of the club-face. The fault is an out-to-in swing path with an open club-face, which imparts slice spin with the straight-face clubs. As the loft of the club increases, that side spin becomes backspin, so that the same swing straightens up the shot with the mid-irons

and lofted woods and pulls the ball left with the short
and steeply lofted clubs.

USEFUL AIDS FROM
THE CLUB MAKERS

When I was a young boy we lived in a tiny apartment
behind the shop at Lindrick Golf Club in Yorkshire and
I used to love hanging around in the workshop watching
my father make clubs and trying to make myself useful
by handing him his tools as he needed them. He died
when I was nine and when I went to grammar school
my mother insisted that I matriculate in woodwork,
on the sensible grounds that it would be a valuable
skill when I turned pro and would have to learn the
club-maker's art.

My first job was as assistant to Willie Wallace, a fine
club-maker who himself had been assistant to the great
J. H. Taylor before the 1914–18 war. During the 1930s
Willie had eight assistants at Hallamshire making clubs
which were exported all over the world.

When I joined him in 1947, during the winter I spent
most of my time making clubs. I adored making woods
and I shall never forget the first set I made. They were
all shafted and gripped, with the heads shaped and the
bone face inserted. Now, after staining and varnishing,
I had to stamp the maker's name on the heads. I went
to great pains, using a set-square, to get the lines exactly
right before bringing the hammer down with a clonk on

to the name die. When I grounded the club I knew it was wrong. Willie immediately noticed my mistake. I had stamped the name exactly at right angles to the club-face.

The name should have been stamped at a slight angle to provide a visual reminder to the player to take the club back along an arc from which he could swing the club into the ball from the inside. In those days some club-makers put yellow bands on the top of woods for the same reason. These days you see some woods (albeit made of metal in most cases) with no names or markings at all on the top. I think that is quite wrong.

For the same reason the bottom edge of iron clubs aims at the target but the top edge of the blade is angled open, progressively more so as you go from three-iron to the wedge. If those two lines were parallel we would subconsciously be inclined to take the club-head straight back. Those angled top edges encourage us to allow the club to move back naturally on an inward arc as we turn our shoulders.

These days golfers have a great advantage in that they can get clubs with specifications which are exactly suitable for them. In our golf schools we stock only two models but they come in a full range of head weights and lies, various shafts and shaft lengths, and grip types and thicknesses can be customised for each individual.

Down the years the trend has been to add more weight to the bottom of the iron clubs in order to assist the handicap golfer to get the ball into the air. I believe it would be better to switch the weight to the top of the blade and take care of the height problem by increasing the loft which is so forgiving of the accidentally imparted side spin that produces slices and hooks. If you contact the ball somewhere near its equator it will go along the ground anyway. That is when I find myself remarking, under my breath, of course: 'Good putt!'

KID YOURSELF

When a golfer is two up with four to play he is tempted to overdo the safety first policy. He takes what he believes to be extra care on every stroke and steers well clear of any possible danger. All too often this pussy-footing policy costs him the match. In this situation try to imagine that you are two down with four to play and suit your tactics accordingly.

It helps me.

Sometimes.

A TIMELY TIP

It was about eleven o'clock at night and I was just on my way up to my Lytham St Annes hotel room when I was approached by a very young, very polite Tony Jacklin.

'Excuse me, Mr Jacobs, but I am off very early in the morning and I wondered if you could possibly take a look at my swing before I go out to play.'

I had watched him play quite a lot and had already

marked him out as a winner, because of his determination and the fact that he had learnt the knack of scoring. But his swing was not quite right, hence the fact that he had only just made the cut in the Pringle tournament, and was therefore allotted a highly unsocial starting time. Two rounds were played on the final day in 1967.

We met very early and when I inspected his clubs I saw grass marks right up in the heel. His problem was that he was standing with his shoulders open at the address and with the ball too far forward. As a result he was taking the club back on too flat a plane into a position from which it was impossible for him to attack the ball from the inside. My remedy was to square up his stance and bring the ball back, putting him in a position from where he could swing the club-head more upright on an in-to-out path and square the club-face by clearing his body.

That day, from being way behind, he shot two great rounds, and won his first tournament.

CUTTING THE LEGS
FROM UNDER HIM

For some years I served on the instructional panel assembled by the American magazine *Golf Digest*, alongside such luminaries of the game as Sam Snead, Paul Runyan, Cary Middlecoff, Dr Gary Wiren, Bob Toski and Jim Flick. One of the magazine's editors would put readers' questions to us and we would all weigh in with our two penn'orth.

At that time, in the sixties, there was a vogue for what was called leg drive and golfers did exercises to strengthen their legs and put more oomph into it as they tried to spring into the shot. There was therefore a hint of heresy in the question which was put to us: 'How important are the legs?' One of the panelists, a most distinguished player and teacher, took it upon himself to define the function and importance of leg-action. In the course of his homily he was severely critical of European golfers and diagnosed their shortcomings as neglect of the legs.

The next question was: 'How important is it for an instructor to be able to demonstrate what he teaches?' I fielded that question and cited the previous speaker as an excellent example of a teacher who practised what he preached. I complimented him warmly on his vivid demonstrations of golfing virtues, such as hitting a full shot from a kneeling position.

'How far do you hit a drive like that?' I enquired.

'About 260 yards,' he replied. The other panelists broke into laughter.

Sam Snead kicked me under the table and muttered: 'You bastard, Jacobs!' That kick was the panel's final contribution on leg-action.

Later I served on a similar panel for *Golf* magazine and there I found a soul mate in Harvey Penick. His approach to teaching golf was utterly practical and down-to-earth and conformed perfectly with my own ideas. I found him also, and more importantly, to be a perfect gentleman in the best senses of that expression.

DOUBLE PAY DAY

Norman von Nida perfectly fits the Australian stereo-
type, a rough, tough, forthright character concealing a
heart the size of Ayers Rock, and I got on exceptionally
well with him, possibly because we Yorkshiremen are
supposed to come from a similar mould. Norman was a
fine player and in September of 1949 he came to Gezira
Sporting Club, where I was the golf pro, to compete in
the Egyptian Match Play Championship.

In the final he met Hassan Hassanein, a brilliant
Sudanese pro who won the Italian and French Open
Championships and who tragically and unaccountably
took his own life by drenching himself in petrol and
striking a match. Hassan, or Doc as he was more famili-
arly called, won that final and in the victory speeches
Norman embarrassed the life out of Rita and me by
castigating the Gezira Club for not allowing us to use
the club's amenities. There was a happy sequel to that
incident because the next day we received a note from
the British ambassador inviting us to use the swimming
pool at the British Embassy any time we liked.

When we moved back to England Norman used to
stay with us at Moor Park and one day we were engaged
to play an exhibition at Hayling Island. Norman was,
and remains to this day, a fanatical horse-racing enthusiast and is well known as a consultant in the highly
technical field of appraising the racing potential of
young thoroughbreds. He had a half share in a horse

45

and in the sixties his partner, Kel Nagle, had the singular – by which I mean double – honour of being presented with the Melbourne Cup by Her Majesty the Queen.

Anyway, as we drove through Ascot that day on the way to Hayling Island Norman remembered he had a hot tip on a horse priced at 12–1 and he must stop and get a bet down. I had no knowledge or interest in racing and completely forgot about the incident until we were driving back home from the exhibition and Norman insisted we stop to find out the fate of his horse. When he came back to the car he pulled out a wad and peeled off twelve of those big, crisp, white fivers and said that while putting a hundred on for himself he had added a fiver to the bet on my behalf. In those days we got £25 for an exhibition match so I rated that one of the best days of my life.

Even better, in retrospect, is the fact that I came out ahead of the gambling game against all the odds because that triumph did not prove habit forming and I never bet on a horse again.

ON THE RUN

At the Carnoustie Open of 1953 I was drawn first off for the Monday qualifying round which all the competitors, even the defending champion, had to play in those days. My playing companion did not turn up for our eight a.m. starting time so the starter, Gerald Micklem, asked me if I would like to play with a marker or wait to pair up with someone else in the same situation.

That could have meant kicking my heels for the whole day so I went off with a lady appointed to mark my card. I was back in the clubhouse at nine-forty, by which time the pair who were second off had still not completed the front nine.

That round does not appear in the *Guinness Book of Records* but I think one hour and forty minutes must constitute the fastest round in the history of the championship. I found it a strange and difficult experience to play by myself because I had to play the ball as soon as I reached it, without the usual luxury of being able to assess the situation at leisure and consider my options while the other chap played his shot.

I scored 77 or 78 and that wasn't as bad as it sounds because it was a vile day, wet and blustery. Anyway, I put together a good enough score next day to qualify for the championship proper.

GET THE PICTURE

Some tournament professionals these days use a wedge for all the little shots around the green and play them very well. But I cannot stress too strongly that this is not the way for ninety-nine per cent of golfers, including Tour players, to play those little chips and pitch shots which are such valuable stroke savers. The routine should be first to examine the lie of the ball, then to look at the flagstick, then to visualise the ball landing on the green and rolling up to the hole, and finally to select the club most suitable to turn that image into reality.

ON THE BOX

My first experience of working for television was at the 1967 Walker Cup match at Royal St George's. The BBC asked me to join the commentary team as the expert analyst alongside Henry Longhurst and Bill Cox. For some reason neither of those two was available for the BBC's next golf commitment, which was coverage of the Daks tournament. So I was pressed into service again, on this occasion with David Coleman.

This time there occurred one of those trivial incidents which you don't think much about at the time but which in retrospect loom as a turning point in a career. Malcolm Gregson was leading the Daks tournament and on the last hole, where he was lying pin-high in two, I could see from his practice swing that he was worried about the way the ball lay for his chip. We couldn't get a close-up of the ball but I was confident enough from the evidence of Gregson's preparations and told the viewers my conclusions.

Gregson won the tournament, enabling him to top the PGA order of merit table that year, and when David Coleman interviewed him he said that he had been very nervous about the lie of his ball for that shot on the last hole.

That comment endorsed my reputation as a pundit

and in due course the BBC offered me a generous contract. Only Henry Longhurst was under contract to the BBC so I felt I had arrived. The trouble was the contract didn't. Weeks passed and no contract came through and in the meantime I bumped into Jimmy Hill, Head of Sport at London Weekend Television. We chatted and next morning a contract from ITV arrived on my desk, very similar to the promised BBC deal and equally lucrative.

I rang Brian Cowgill, Head of BBC Sport, and informed him of this development. The BBC contract arrived post haste. My choice was heavily influenced by ITV's promise of a thirteen-part teaching series. We made this in three and a half days at Moortown, having invited public participation. Many golfers turned up and I selected thirteen of them, each with a different fault which would form the basis of one of the programmes. By using the split-screen technique we were able to show the Before and After swings of each individual and the series proved so popular that we eventually made thirty-nine of those programmes.

They led to a thirteen-part series of target golf for which I devised concrete saucers as water hazards of different sizes at different distances, the splashes providing unequivocal evidence of the direct hits and adding to the visual interest of the pictures. I was also involved in a series at the exotic West Indian location of the Lucayan Country Club with the likes of Jack Nicklaus and Billy Casper.

These instructional ventures were immensely satisfying to me, and excellent publicity for my teaching practice as well, but the tournament work for ITV was a different matter. Many times I had occasion to wonder if I should have stayed with the BBC.

The problem with the commercial networks was that trade union rules insisted that the region where a tournament was being played had to supply the production team of director, cameramen and all the ancillary crew of riggers, fitters, drivers and so on.

Televising golf is a highly specialised business and over the years the BBC had assembled a team of experienced golfing experts who knew the game through and through and who therefore produced programmes of the highest technical quality and smooth efficiency. The crew assembled for an ITV regional tournament, on the other hand, might be headed by a director whose professional forte was the ballet and who knew nothing of golf. Even the best of these directors had little chance, covering golf so seldom. When the camera work was so poor, we commentators were often made to look stupid, a most galling experience for men who were employed specifically to display their wisdom.

ROLE REVERSAL

Golf axiom: in mixed foursomes all husbands become golf professionals. During one tournament I could stand the hectoring and bullying no longer and enquired of the lady how on earth she could put up with being addressed in such terms by her husband. 'Oh, he's not my husband,' she assured me, 'he's my lover.'

THE VITAL PRELIMINARY

Most faults originate in an address position from which it is impossible to make a good swing. It happens quite frequently that a golfer will come to me in despair and, after putting him into a good address position, he will immediately hit one beautiful shot after another without any further advice. With professionals and low-handicap amateurs, a single word, such as 'Posture!', will often do the trick.

Sometimes speech is unnecessary and the tip of the forefinger pressed gently on the right shoulder, accompanied by a conspiratorial wink, will constitute the entire lesson by conveying a reminder to keep the upper body square to the line of the shot at the address. It is more than half the battle in golf to get those two positions – the aim of the club and the address – right. That is why I like to send my pupils away with the battlecry: 'Set it up and set it off and leave the rest to the good Lord.'

A WORD IN SEASON

One of my failures was the brilliantly gifted Irish amateur, Joe Carr. In retrospect I should never have tried
to impose my ideas on the glorious exuberance of his
whirling dervish style. Whatever he lacked in ortho-
doxy he more than made up for in innate talent and
competitive spirit, sufficient to win some twenty-six
championships. We both did our best but soon mutually
decided to leave well alone. I reverted to being just one
of his million or so friends.

Another of this legion of friends was the Dublin Chief
of Police who was also a fellow member of Sutton Golf
Club. One evening Joe was driving home at a fair lick,
and in braking for some traffic lights his car skidded on
the wet road and slid slap into the back of a police car.
The two officers got out and when they recognised Joe
they apologised for the necessity of having to do their
bounden duty but in view of the damage to the police
car they would have to take full details and report the
incident. Joe said sure and he understood perfectly that
the officers had no choice in the matter.

The next morning the Chief of Police dropped in to
Sutton Golf Club for his customary cup of coffee and
Joe recounted what had happened. The Chief of Police
telephoned the local station and said: 'I understand
that last night one of your lads backed into a friend
of mine . . .'

REVEALED: THE SECRET
OF LONG HITTING

Everyone wants to hit the ball a long way and I am often asked for the secret. As often as not when I say 'Club-head speed correctly applied' I can detect that the enquirer suspects I am holding something back, as if the initiation ceremony into the Professional Golfers' Association included the passing on of some long-hitting formula which the novice pro must swear on his life never to disclose. As it happens I was for a while a long hitter and I will now make a full revelation of what I believe gave me the ability to hit the ball harder.

As a boy I used to work horses in the fields alongside the first and fourth holes of Lindrick Golf Club. I was paid at the rate of half a crown for mowing four greens. When the threshing machine came around for the annual task of winnowing the neighbouring farmer's corn from the sheaves of wheat and oats and barley, my task was to work the 'clean' end of the machine (as opposed to the 'dirty' end which spewed out the straw and chaff and dust). I had to bag up and weigh the grain and then carry the 18-stone sacks up a flight of rickety steps and stack them in the granary.

A full day's work at this chore represented a fair session of body building and helped make me as strong as a bull. I recommend it to anyone who really wants to follow my example, witnessed by my cousin Jack, of once driving pin-high at the 400-yard first hole at Lindrick, albeit aided, as if you had not already guessed, by a following wind of gale force and a very hard fairway.

THE FLOP WEDGE

There has recently been a vogue for carrying three wedges: pitching wedge, sand wedge and flop wedge of sixty degrees or more loft. I think this is an excellent idea and have done so for fifty years or so. The reasons I discarded the two-iron in favour of a third wedge were that I could play the ball back in my stance and hit a two-iron shot with the three-iron so it was easy enough to create a vacancy in my bag.

I have always been a believer in a close graduation of distances in the shorter clubs because it is more difficult to play half and three-quarter shots close to the green. So it is always better to play a full shot into the green, hence the value of having a larger range of clubs to accommodate smaller graduations in distances.

MY PROUDEST ACHIEVEMENT

When I took on the task of setting up an independent European professional golf tour to replace the rather haphazard and hand-to-mouth promotion of small-scale British tournaments by the Professional Golfers' Association, I found myself embroiled in the most acrimonious disputes between club professionals and the new breed of tournament specialists.

This was internecine war of intense bitterness and a strong feeling developed among the professional golfers, as opposed to the golf professionals, that they should make a clean break and form their own separate organisation. I was determined that this should not happen and battled away to create a strong and permanent bond between the two branches of professional golf.

After a great struggle I obtained agreement for an executive committee consisting of three tournament players and three club professionals. It was clearly essential that this committee should have a strong, independent chairman. I was delighted that the man I felt best fitted for this difficult and delicate challenge agreed to take it on. Michael Bonallack did a wonderful job, just as he has subsequently made an outstanding success of the most important job in the world of golf, as secretary of the Royal & Ancient Golf Club of St Andrews.

As a player he smashed all the records in amateur golf, despite being one of the most extreme up-and-under tilters of my experience. But he was also one of the greatest up-and-downers I have known. The American wisecrack about being able to get up and down from the ball washer might have been coined for Michael. His putting was positively inspired.

Altogether he is a super golfer and a super guy and I shall always be grateful to him for his invaluable help at a critical time in the affairs of pro golf.

Looking back over a long and full life I think that the delicate and intractable task of securing a reconciliation and an enduring partnership within the profession is the proudest achievement of my career.

IN A WORLD OF SLICERS
THE HOOKER IS KING

Most of the great players are fighting a hook. So in their ghosted instruction articles for the golf magazines they tend to advocate a weaker grip than normal, that is with both hands rotated anti-clockwise combined with a late hit.

The effect of this expert anti-hook instruction being disseminated to a world of slicers can be easily imagined. The slicers get worse and flock to me and the other teachers in droves. I am not complaining, mind. I have always appreciated the time and effort the superstars put in to drum up business for me.

Some of those magazine readers whose fades have been converted into vicious slices by following the wise advice of the star players ask me: 'How do I get a late hit?'

I counter with my stock reply: 'What is wrong with hitting at the right time?' End of discussion.

HOPELESS CASES

The only people whose golf cannot be improved are those who won't listen.

A GAME FOR A LIFETIME

The best thing about golf is the handicapping system. It means that everyone, young or old, learner or expert, can compete against each other on level terms. And with suitable handicap adjustments you can go on playing golf and competing until the day you become a divot.

WIDER STILL AND WIDER

Peter Alliss was a wonderful player. He was a fantastic iron player and an excellent chipper and pitcher. He comes from a golfing family, of course, and he inherited from his father, Percy, the rather patronising title of 'the best golfer never to have won an Open Championship'. For most of his career, which was distinguished enough in all conscience, the one part of his game which did not match the rest was his driving. He had a strong grip and he was rather narrow in his backswing.

He came to stay with me when he played in the Esso round robin tournament at Moor Park and we worked on that slightly stilted backswing. I made him make a full turn away from the ball. It was a good time to introduce this extra width into his swing because the tournament was match play and in this form of golf you feel you can let yourself go and give it a good rip whereas stroke play inhibits experiments.

He has since said that he played the best golf of his life that week. We can only speculate on what he might have achieved if a twitchy putter had not forced his early retirement.

WHEN DID YOU LAST COUNT YOUR KNUCKLES?

It really makes no difference whether you use an overlapping grip, an interlocking grip or a two-handed grip, just provided both hands work in harmony. Nor does it matter how many knuckles you can see when you address the ball. For example, if you have a three-knuckle grip at the address position but turn it into a one-knuckle grip in the hitting area you will obviously hook the ball, and vice versa. There is no point in trying to count your knuckles at impact as you make a full swing. Just watch the flight of the ball. If you are doing everything else correctly – and you will almost certainly need a competent instructor to confirm this point – and the ball is still hooking or slicing, then the cause must lie with a faulty grip. And the only definition of a correct grip is one that consistently delivers the club-face square to the line of shot.

IN PURSUIT OF GOLF'S
HOLY GRAIL

In one respect golf resembles a swan gliding regally across a mill pond. To the spectators at a championship it all looks so effortless and natural but that is an illusion. A formidable effort of concentration must be applied on a specific aspect of technique for each swing, just as the swan's legs must drive hard, out of sight.

Since success is the result of hard work and technical improvement, it follows that golfers will be tempted to seek even greater success through even harder work and searching for more improvements. Ben Hogan, Byron Nelson, Gary Player, Roberto de Vicenzo and Arnold Palmer come to mind as players who have made radical changes after having already achieved substantial success. And, of course, Nick Faldo. To my mind, his courage and winner's temperament together with his superb short game are his greatest assets. Strangely, although Faldo's technical adjustments are plainly substantial in his mind, they are not particularly obvious to the onlooker. But the continuing search for perfection is clearly important to him.

Tom Watson got so close to perfection that, in his words, he could smell it, before he was forced to accept what most of us hold to be a universal truth of golf, that the greatest of champions will make occasional mistakes and the only thing to do is shrug them off and concentrate on the next shot.

Nick is not ready to adopt such a policy of despair. He still has his vision and the rich successes to justify it. The slightest error transfixes him like the thrust of a dagger and reinforces his determination to improve. My own involvements in that process were successful enough but they were remedial in nature, changing the plugs when his game was misfiring, and I never had an opportunity to give him a complete engine overhaul. For that he selected David Leadbetter and in doing so he made a wise choice.

Nick wanted continuity and constant fine tuning, a concept quite alien to my background and beliefs. Players of my generation were generous in sound advice, when asked, but for the most part they knew their own swings and how to put them right when things went wrong. The idea of a personal coach in constant attendance would have struck them very oddly indeed. As for the notion of consulting a sports psychologist, anyone who contemplated such a course of action would, as the old joke has it, need his head examining.

But times change and, if scoring standards improve, we must accept that they are changing for the better. Jack Nicklaus has had a huge impact on professional golf and his example changed it fundamentally, in several ways. I suspect that Nick might prove to be a similar trend setter for young recruits to the game. Being a hero figure puts a heavy responsibility on a champion sportsman, as I am sure he understands. I might even suggest that it is more important than mastering the perfect swing.

AN ENJOYABLE AND A
SPECIAL RELATIONSHIP

The start of my enduring love affair with the United States was in 1955 when I went over to play the American circuit, the highlight of which was a fortuitous pairing with Byron Nelson at Thunderbird in Palm Springs where we were to have the Ryder Cup match. In that match I acquitted myself well enough, two points from two matches, to earn invitations for the Masters for the next two years. Can you believe that I declined each time with regrets that my lesson book was too full?

In 1972 I heard from an old friend, Ken Bowden, co-editor of my book, *Practical Golf,* and now editor of *Golf Digest* magazine. He invited me to preside over the magazine's first golf school on Phoenix, Arizona. A number of American professionals came along as observers. Afterwards Bert Beuhler, Shelby Futch, Craig and Scott Bunker and the English pro Donald (Doon) Crawley joined me in the creation of the first John Jacobs Practical Golf Schools. They are still with us, veterans of a teaching corps of more than 120 professionals. We all worked like mad but we still had fun. For example, there was our annual Ryder Cup match when Doon Crawley and I, representing Europe, played two of the US staff.

It was exciting and exacting work building up the 24 locations for the John Jacobs Golf Schools (more than 1,000 classes are scheduled in 1995). When the toil and travel became too taxing for me, Shelby, to my great good fortune, stepped in and took over the reins as my partner and later as the owner of the company. I am extremely proud of all those guys who worked so hard helping me build up the business. I owe so much to them, and to America.

THE ETERNAL
FUNDAMENTALS

A STEP-BY-STEP GUIDE
TO GREAT GOLF

Golf is what the ball does. What the ball does is determined by what the club-head is doing when it hits it. To be successful, then, we have to be able to control the impact of the club and the ball in the following dimensions:

The club-face, *which can only be square, open or closed at impact.*

The club swing path, *which can only be straight through, in-to-out or out-to-in at impact.*

The angle of approach *of the club to the ball must be correct. A little explanation: a driver for which the ball is teed up is hit after the club has passed the bottom of the arc, i.e. on the upswing (for the best players one to three degrees). This angle of attack is unworkable when the ball is sitting on bare turf when the blow has to be a descending one.*

The speed of the club. *How far and how straight the ball will go is dependent on club-head speed correctly applied, i.e. correct Face, correct Path, correct Angle.*

Your best chance of applying the club correctly is to start your swing from a position which makes the correct impact probable. I often think I have spent my life putting people into a position from which they can hit the ball.

That position starts with a grip which will bring the club-face square at impact.

The club is aimed by placing it behind the ball with the sole grounded and the shaft in a vertical plane so that the loft on the club is what the maker intended. This establishes the feet position relative to the ball.

You must take a stance which allows the upper part of the body to be square to the club-face.

This aim and stance give the best chance of swinging the club through the ball in the right direction.

Lastly the correct posture at address must be adopted: head up, knees flexed and a reasonably straight back make it possible to swing on the correct arc and therefore achieve the correct angle of attack.

So, dear reader, although impact has to be fairly precise, do not worry about that. Swing the club on an arc which suits the situation whereby the ball is to the side of you and it is on the ground.

The hands and arms swing the club up and down because the ball is on the ground, at the same time that the body turns. So the club swings from in-to-in as well as up and down. Whether you consciously swing the club on the in-to-in arc and the body moves out of the way to make this possible, or you consciously turn the body to make room for the correct arc, matters little. The dear Lord made fantastic human beings. If you start from the correct address and with the right posture He will do the rest.

There we have what might be termed the iron rations of golf instruction, the bare essentials. The American amateur, Bobby Jones, was not only an extraordinarily gifted player but when he retired he became a highly respected teacher of the game. The secret of imparting written instruction, he felt, was to repeat the basic messages over and over again in different forms. For example, in seeking to convey the sensation of the swing, an exhortation to 'drive a tack into the back of the ball' may fall on uncomprehending ears, whereas the same message expressed as 'feel you are swinging a bucket of water without spilling a drop' will offer a ray of enlightenment. So, it can do no harm and may be of benefit if we recap the gospel of golf.

Always remember that it is the ball that plays the golf. You may have the prettiest swing in the world but unless the ball goes to the right places you are not a good golfer. All that matters in golf is the relationship between the ball and the club-face. Think of yourself as the servant of the club-face, anxious to do the bidding of the partnership between ball and club-face. All they ask of you is to obey five orders:

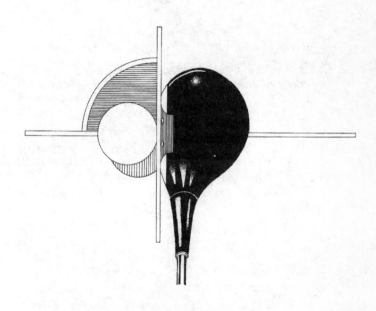

1 Deliver the club-face square to the line of the shot at impact.

2 Contrive to swing the club-head so that at impact it is travelling directly along the line towards the target.

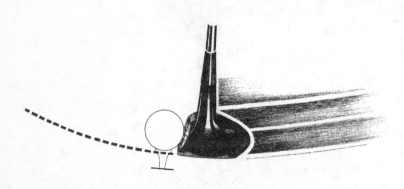

3 The club-head must approach the ball at the most effective angle of attack.

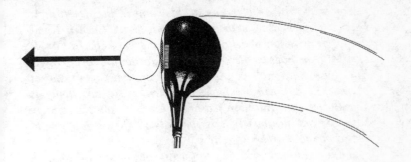

4 Meet the ball flush in the centre of the club-face.

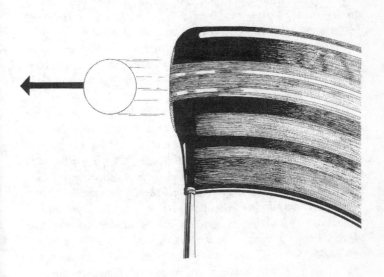

5 Deliver the club-head at speed.

Perform those simple, menial tasks correctly, using whatever method you care to adopt (provided you can repeat it consistently), and you will be a champion.

You may raise an objection at this point in the proceedings: I am a mere mortal, with human limitations. Even if I had the foggiest notion of what comprises the most effective angle of attack, or how to present the club-face square to the target line, I am incapable of thinking of more than one thing at a time. At a pinch I might give attention to two thoughts simultaneously. But don't ask me to focus on five critical subjects simultaneously. It is impossible. The attempt would reduce me to a gibbering wreck.

That would never do. I do not want you consciously to think about any of those five imperatives during the swing. Actually, there is a school of thought which says that thinking about how to make a good swing is a sure guarantee of ruining a good swing. Therefore you should occupy your mind with some completely irrelevant thought, like sex or income tax. And I must admit that in my time I have known a number of fine players who broke course records while their minds were occupied exclusively with erotic fantasies. My feeling is that there are productive thoughts which enhance the pleasures and the performance of golf, of which more anon, but none of them concerns how to swing the club.

We can take care of those five imperatives by the way we prepare to play the stroke. Do I hear a gasp of surprise and delight at this assurance? That is the very word I use to remind my pupils of the undoubted fact that the fate of a golf shot is settled before the ball is struck. GASP is the acronym which holds the secret of good golf, as will shortly be revealed.

I sometimes do a little party trick when I am with a friend at a practice range. As we stroll behind the line of practising golfers I will remark, 'Here comes a slice,' or 'Duck hook.' I am not being immodest when I say that I am rarely wrong; it is not difficult to forecast the result when you have spent most of your adult life studying the faults of golfers. In the same way, it helps the process of teaching golf if the teacher can quickly establish his credibility.

Many beginners are resistant to teaching. They harbour this idea that it is all very well for him to pontificate about the Vardon grip but he doesn't know how I feel and I know for sure that a two-handed grip is the only way for me. So another party trick can come in handy to break down that attitude. I stand with my back to the pupil, facing down the range, and ask him to hit a shot. I observe the flight of the ball and tell him what he is doing wrong. It might be: 'You are standing with your shoulders open,' or 'You are not completing your backswing.' It would be quite possible, if slightly anti-social, to conduct an entire lesson without looking at what the pupil is doing but simply watching the flight of his shots and correcting his errors. One of the objectives of my teaching is to give the pupil this ability to diagnose his own faults from the behaviour of the ball and to apply the necessary remedy.

All this arises from GASP, the very fountain from which springs good golf.

G is for grip
Millions of words have been written and uttered on the subject of holding a golf club. Maybe you have been the unfortunate victim of this spate of verbiage and your mind is spinning with notions of holding tubes of toothpaste, or live birds, or increasing the pressure of your left pinkie through the impact zone. If so, please remember that the only function of the grip is to return the club-face square to the ball at speed. If it achieves that it does not matter whether you use an overlap, interlock, baseball grip or even hold the club with the left hand below the right.

A is for aim
Watch how a great professional golfer sets about the task of making a shot. Having first looked down the line and taken his grip, he places the club-head very deliberately behind the ball. There are some who do this with only one hand on the

Fig.1 *You must have a grip which consistently returns the club-face square to the ball.*

Fig. 2 *Sight the target, and picture the shot in your mind.*

72

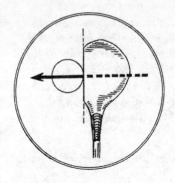

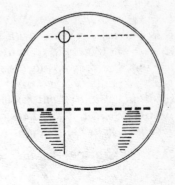

Fig. 3 *Place the club-head behind the ball with the club-face exactly square to your target line.*

Fig. 4 *Soling the club-head establishes the ball position relative to the feet.*

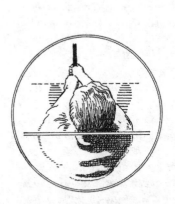

Fig. 5 *Correct ball position makes possible good shoulder alignment.*

Fig. 6 *Correct posture leads to correct shoulder turn.*

73

club but this is not to be recommended. If only the left hand is used the ball tends to be positioned too far forward and, conversely, if the club is held with the right hand only the ball gets too far back. With infinite care he positions the club so that the sole is resting flush on the turf and the leading edge of the club-face, NOT the top edge, mind, is precisely square to the target line. Individual routines vary in detail, of course, but commonly the aim of the club-head fixes the shaft and will therefore determine where to position your feet relative to the ball.

S is for stance – *which includes square shoulder alignment.*

The aiming of the club has necessitated a slight stooping over the ball and now the golfer straightens his back while maintaining a degree of flexion in the knees. This directly leads to correct posture.

P is for posture

When you adopt this routine, and follow it with the zeal of a religious fanatic on every shot, you will automatically answer some of the commonest questions asked by beginners, such as 'How close should I stand to the ball?' By positioning the club and then moving on to it you have the answer. 'Where should I place my feet in relation to the ball?' is another regular query. That routine takes care of the answer.

If you ask the average club member what is the most important thing in the golf swing the probability is that you will get the reply: 'Keep your head down.' That advice is probably as old as golf itself, handed down from the original shepherds knocking pebbles into rabbit holes with their crooks. Or whoever was responsible for originating this exasperating and entrancing pastime. And wherever that invention may have been made. Mary, Queen of Scots may well have been exhorted to keep her head down, and almost certainly that was the last exhortation she heard on this earth, from the lips of the headsman as she rested her chin on the block. 'Keep your head down' has kept me in lucrative employment for nearly fifty years. Keeping your head down is a sure way of ruining the shot. March into battle behind the banner emblazoned 'Keep your head UP' and victory shall be yours. If your head is down your swing will be too straight, with dire consequences. Keep your head up and your club will go back on the most effective swing plane for a good shot.

So now you are set, knees slightly flexed, back straight and inclined forward, head up, eyes down and focused on the ball, arms hanging down from the shoulders, the back of your left hand almost brushing the inside of your left thigh, right shoulder slightly dropped to accommodate the placing of your right hand below the left. Above all, check the paramount condition for despatching your ball directly at the target: the alignment of the feet, the thighs, the waist and the shoulders must be parallel to the target line.

This routine is quicker to do than to describe. But there is no time limit involved in setting yourself up to the ball. Until the routine becomes second nature, as it quickly will, you should go through a check drill like the captain of a jumbo jet making absolutely certain that everything is in proper trim for take-off. Get everything right and you will have taken care of most of those five imperatives demanded by your master, the club-face.

*Keeping your head down induces a TILT of the shoulders
and too straight an upswing arc. The tilter's rocking and
blocking action produces inconsistent shot-making and
can cause lower-back problems.*

Standing tall and proud with your head up, the upper body just slightly inclined from the hips, enables you to TURN the shoulders, thus setting the club in the correct plane and direction without putting strain on the spine. Good posture obviates any danger of rock and block.

THE BACK NINE

THE CRADLE OF THE GAME

Scotland is the only country in the world which has enough golf courses to satisfy the natural demand for golf. The country is rightly proud of its history as the cradle of golf and the centre of the world's governing body. Children pick up the game naturally and I suppose that if there were an international competition for hundred-strong teams of teenagers Scotland would walk it every time. But these youngsters do not progress and develop into great champions. (Yes, I am well aware of Sandy Lyle's credentials as a champion but I am not totally convinced about his credentials as a Scot. Certainly he is not a product of the Scottish way of golf.)

Scotland has not had a home-born and home-based champion for one hundred years and that is odd for a country which produces such a profusion of talented youngsters. There may be harsh economic realities which demand that teenagers must get into employment and become bread-winners as soon as possible but I believe that further progress in the game is also arrested by an attitude of mind. They set little or no store by formal lessons, seemingly believing themselves to have been born with a thorough knowledge of technique as a genetic inheritance, along with a pawky sense of humour and a predeliction for strong drink. I have encountered open hostility to suggestions that expert tuition would be beneficial.

In its way this mind-set is as damaging as the old English tradition of amateur sport which decreed that practice, be it for golf or cricket or any other sporting activity, was tantamount to cheating. Not the done thing, old boy. That prejudice was a casualty of the Second World War, greatly to the benefit of English sport, and now I detect a more receptive attitude in Scotland to the teaching of golf. I think that the great Scottish amateur, Charlie Green, has been influential in spreading the gospel of expert tuition, and the international success of Bob Torrance as coach to many great players, in addition to his own son, Sam, has helped the cause. As a result I expect to see Scotland resume its traditional production of great champions.

HALE – AND HEARTY
AT FORTY-EIGHT

Once when I arrived at our golf school in Scottsdale, Arizona, the staff told me that I had just missed Hale Irwin. He had been there two weeks practising for six hours a day and he had hit every single shot with his feet together. Hale has always had a tendency to swing a little flat and had adopted this feet-together drill to restore the feeling of swinging his hands and arms up and under rather than around his body. Not long after, at Medinah in 1990, he won his third U.S. Open Championship, aged 48.

Bernhard Langer's largely self-taught swing was exceptionally flat. It is also exceptionally effective, but with all personal idiosyncrasies there is a tendency for that individual quirk to become exaggerated to the point, unless checked, of self-parody and even self-destruction. So I was alert to that danger when he approached me as a young man during a tournament at the RAC Club, Epsom, and asked politely: 'What would you do with my swing, Mr Jacobs?'

I asked him to look on me as his best girl, admittedly an exercise involving a considerable flight of the imagination, and then I stationed myself behind him and slightly to the side in a position where he would have to raise his arms on the backswing in order to avoid hitting me in the face with his club-head. (I used the girlfriend metaphor for emphasis but there is really no reason to put your loved ones in physical danger in order to correct a flat swing plane. Position yourself near a hedge or something soft like that for this exercise.)

Another remedial treatment for an excessively flat swing is to find a suitable slope and practise with the ball below the level of your feet. This situation demands that the hands go higher in the backswing in order to reach the ball in the downswing. The converse also applies if your swing is too straight instead of being an in-to-in arc. Hitting shots with the ball positioned above the feet gets the body turning instead of tilting, which makes room for the correct arc.

WHAT DO YOU MEAN –
LEG DRIVE?

My good friend and former business partner, Laddie
Lucas, was possibly the best left-handed amateur golfer
in the history of the game and I am not overlooking Phil
Mickelson in making that judgment. His brother-in-law
was the late Douglas Bader, the war hero who became
a fighter ace despite having lost both legs in a pre-war
flying accident.

The Lucas children were out playing when Father
passed on a word of advice: 'You'll never hit the ball
a long way unless you drive through with the legs.'

'What about Uncle Douglas?' came the prompt reply.
'He hits it farther than anybody.'

Game, set and match.

SPLIT DECISION

Expert witnesses are immensely popular in legal circles, not for the value of their evidence but because they prolong the proceedings and keep the lawyers' fees accumulating. The reason expert evidence is ineffective is because when the eminent expert for the plaintiff has given his evidence the defence calls an equally eminent expert to testify to the exact contrary.

Expert golf tuition can get a bit like that, as I discovered when Mark McCormack came to me for a refresher. This was shortly after he had set up his golf management business, so the rust had only just begun to erode what had been a pretty effective amateur swing. It was also the period when leg-action was all the rage. Mark had fallen into the habit of locking his arms to his shoulders and swinging himself, instead of the club, from the top of the backswing.

Having explained the whys and wherefores of his problem to him, I had him address the ball with his feet together, to discourage his tendency to lunge from the top, and gave him the battlecry: 'Point the club, use the club,' to reinforce the message of swinging his arms. He immediately started to hit the ball very nicely and off he went to partner his client, Arnold Palmer, in the Bing Crosby pro–am at Pebble Beach.

Palmer was aghast at the sight of the new Mark McCormack with his narrow stance. 'Plant your feet wide apart so you have a solid base to swing from,' he growled.

Quite soon afterwards Mark had occasion to play with another of his clients, Jack Nicklaus. 'You'll never play good golf with a stance as wide as that,' he said. 'You'll lock the bottom half of your body and restrict the movement of the top half as well. Stand with your feet in a neutral position, just about shoulder width.'

Three experts, three different versions of the holy writ of golf. From such profusion comes confusion.

LET IT HAPPEN

You play your best golf by letting your swing just happen, not by concentrating on making it happen.

Golf instruction often creates over-control. So the mood of a swing should be to 'set it up' (that is, to take a correct address position), 'set it off' (swing the club up to a position from which you can hit the ball) and 'let it freewheel'.

WORLD TOUR

I have known many professional golfers and the vast majority of them have been decent, honest, straight-dealing men. The very nature of a game which is based on honesty and trust, and is unplayable unless these ethical standards are observed, tends to eliminate the bad hats.

I am proud to have spent my life within this brother-hood of professional golfers. Likewise, professional golf is respected as a clean, honest sport and the reason for that enduring reputation, I am quite sure, is that, unlike some other spectator sports, pro golf is run by the players themselves.

When I was invited to become what the newspapers insisted on calling the Supremo of tournament golf, I demanded a completely free hand, without having to refer back to some committee or other, but I recognised that my job was simply to create a structure. Beyond that, I was to be the servant of professional golf, not the master. The players must be in charge.

My other guiding principle was that the public, and the sponsors, and the television companies and other media must be given value for their money. That meant, among other things, having good players and keeping them. We therefore made a rule that members of the Tour must not take part in events which conflicted with our tournaments.

I had to point out this rule to Mark McCormack when

some of the players under contract to him were engaged to compete in a pro–am in Switzerland. Mark told me that they must honour their obligations to the pro–am. I replied that if they did so they would be fined the equivalent of the first prize. For the most part Mark, whom I liked and trusted, was a valuable ally in getting the Tour started.

I was immensely fortunate in that I knew most of the people who ran the national golf federations in continental Europe because of my teaching association with them, so I naturally sought to broaden the base and the playing opportunities by creating a European Tour, rather than simply upgrading the extremely rudimentary British golf circuit. And how that has paid off! It is impossible to over-emphasise the effect Seve Ballesteros had on the growth of the European Tour by the way he changed the whole outlook of the European players. Sixteen major championships and two and a half Ryder Cups in the space of fourteen years was the reward for their self-belief inspired by Seve.

When I handed over to Ken Schofield I stressed my belief in the players running their own affairs. He agreed, and what a marvellous job he has done in implementing the wishes of his players and expanding the European Tour.

My experience in the field of golf administration naturally flavours my reaction to suggestions for a world tour. Professional golf is in a healthy state and I am optimistic, confident even, about its future prospects. But I recognise the potential benefits which could accrue from a world tour, always provided that it is done properly. By that I mean that it must be done according to the principles I have outlined above: under the sanction and the authority of the players and by giving value for money to the sponsors and public.

TV can do a great service to sport but it cannot run sport. So I would like to see the five international professional tours getting together with the commercial interests behind the world tour proposals and working out an arrangement which, above all, safeguards the integrity of the sport and which keeps authority over the world tour firmly in the hands of the players.

GO FOR IT

José Maria Olazabal is one of the toughest competitors I have ever known. When he has confidence in his game and gets into a position from which he can win, you can rely on him not to falter and not to miss a shot. Nine times out of ten that means he goes on to win. But Jack Nicklaus and Tom Watson won major championships when they were not at their best and I have been trying to get Olazabal to believe he can win when his game is not one hundred per cent. After all, nobody ever played a round of golf hitting every shot perfectly, or anything like it.

TAKE IT EASY

You should always practise the full swing with a relatively easy club. I used to wear out six-irons on the practice ground. A television director who had just taken up golf asked if I would take a look at his swing. I agreed and when I met him on the practice ground he had a collection of the oldest balls you ever saw and a two-iron. Obviously he did not hit that two-iron very well. None of us plays his best golf with a two-iron.

Later that day while I was doing my television commentary Brian Barnes fluffed a bunker shot and the ball moved about two feet. I remarked: 'That reminds me of our director's two-iron.'

A voice in my headphones came back immediately: 'You're fired!'

BOOED AT ST ANDREWS

The 1955 Open Championship was blessed with balmy sunshine. The Old Course at St Andrews was playing hard and fast, the way a links course should. I had started

70, 71 and, so far as John Jacobs was concerned, God was in His heaven and all was right with the world. I was not so naive as to start anticipating events, but I was doing all right and knew that if I could just keep it going, well . . . who knows what might happen?

My second shot to the seventeenth green finished on a slight downslope just short of the Road Hole bunker. I surveyed the situation carefully, noting the flag position and scanning how much green I had to work with, assessing the chances of recovery if my ball went over the green on to the road (cobbled in those days as opposed to the effete Tarmac of today). I allowed myself a quick glance at the sea of hard-eyed, calculating faces of the spectators crowded behind the wall.

The Scots have a well-deserved reputation for being the most discerning golf watchers in the world, and applause sounds much sweeter when it comes from people who can recognise and appreciate the distinction between a standard shot and a good shot. But at times like this those knowing Scottish galleries can take on the aura of a jury at a murder trial. I knew well enough that if this had been a quiet Saturday evening and I were playing for half a crown with a friend, I could nip the ball right up to the flag. The spectators understood as much, too. But this was the Open Championship and I needed to finish 4,4 to go into the last round in second place, right in contention, challenging for the Open title.

There was a low, guttural murmuring of disapproval as I set myself to chip in a direction well wide of the line to the flag. The gallery's derisive mumbling at my fainthearted decision, or what I would prefer to call endorsement of the notion that discretion is the better part of valour, degenerated into outright booing as I clipped the ball up to the front of the green.

I now faced an enormous putt with a deceptively severe right-to-left swing, presenting a risk – as Brian Barnes demonstrated most famously on a more recent occasion – of putting into the Road Hole bunker. I holed that huge putt – and a detonation of applause from behind the wall signalled the rehabilitation of John Jacobs in the estimation of the world's most knowledgeable crowd.

Eventually there was to be no happy ending. As usual I came a cropper in the final round, taking seven at the fourteenth.

DRAWING (THE BALL) IS BETTER THAN LOSING (THE BALL)

When I was a boy playing Rugby and trying to convert a try, I used to kick the ball with the toe of the boot, like everyone else. These days most Rugby players have changed kicking into a side-on game. They get greater power and accuracy by approaching from an oblique angle and kicking with the inside of the boot and imparting draw on the ball. Footballers also favour the side-on technique for bending free kicks and corners by kicking with the inside of the boot and putting draw on the ball.

Golf is the complete side-on game and because the path of the club-head is from the inside, to square at impact, and then back inside, there is a natural tendency for the club-face to be closing through impact. So the very fact that golf is a side-on game means that the

standard shot is a slight draw. This is not a fault; it is
the natural state of affairs which maximises length and
accuracy. Once that natural shot has been achieved with
consistency, then you may wish to fade the ball or, in
football terms, use the outside of the boot.

If anyone is in doubt about the swing being in-back-
to-in he should observe how the divots of most good
shots certainly point left, since they are taken after the
ball has been struck. That demonstrates how soon the
club returns to the inside path.

OUR CUP RUNNETH OVER

The growth of the Ryder Cup match into one of the
world's premier sporting occasions, right up there
alongside Wimbledon and the Cup Final, has been one
of the most exciting and satisfying developments of my
golfing life. The long domination of the matches by the
Americans, which turned the Ryder Cup into more of a
ceremonial ritual than a valid sporting contest, ended
with the introduction of continental players into what
became the European team.

With my long experience of coaching European
players, and then being instrumental in establishing
the European Tour, I was particularly gratified to be
appointed as captain of that first European Ryder Cup
team, to play the Americans at The Greenbrier, West
Virginia, in 1979. Seve Ballesteros and Tony Garrido
were the only two continentals to make the team and,
as it worked out, their contribution to the points tally

was minimal in the foursomes and the four-balls. Even so, there was only one point in it, in favour of the home team, with twelve singles to play. Clearly, we had a chance of pulling off an historic first victory on American soil.

Mark James who had pulled a muscle on the first morning, was therefore unable to take any further part in the match. The procedure for such a contingency is that both captains put the name of a nominee into a sealed envelope before the match. So now the American envelope had to be opened to reveal the name of the player who would stand down and be deemed to have played a halved match with the injured James. A rather shamefaced American PGA official approached me and said that the American captain, Billy Casper, had unaccountably misunderstood the system and had put the name of his star player, Lee Trevino, instead of his weakest member, into the envelope. Would it be acceptable to the European team for Casper to change his selection?

I called a team meeting, explained the situation and put my case, that we still had a good chance of winning and that I would not want such a victory to be gained on a technicality or tainted by any suggestion of poor sportsmanship. The team agreed and the off-form Gil Morgan was substituted as the envelope man.

The rampaging Trevino inspired the Americans to what looks on paper to have been an easy victory although four of the matches were desperately close and might easily have gone the other way if I had insisted on the rule being followed and our players being given an easier task as a result.

I have questioned my decision many times since but I do not regret it, even though I can think of other captains who would have insisted on the letter of the law, just as I can think of other officials who would not have sought a substitution.

It so happened that two years later, when I captained the team again for the match at Walton Heath, I became aware of another procedural situation which should perhaps be regularised.

Bernard Gallacher was all square with Bill Rogers when they came to the last green. Rogers putted first, his ball finishing two to three inches from the cup; inadvertently he leant forward and raked his ball back to him. Bernard, to his credit, did not claim the hole, asking Rogers to replace the ball which had come to rest behind the hole from where Bernard was putting. The hole and the match, which Bernard could have claimed on a technicality (viz. that a player must not assume a 'gimme' until a putt has been demonstrably conceded), were duly halved.

Regrettably holes have been claimed in similar circumstances which in my view is very much against the spirit of the game so wonderfully personified by Jack Nicklaus at Birkdale in 1969.

GOLF'S WORST DOUBLE ACT, ROCKER AND BLOCKER

On my regular visits to Spain to teach the professionals how to teach, I needed pupils in order to demonstrate and, as often as not, boy caddies were used for this purpose.

I must confess that I have no recollection of the incident, but they tell me that in one of my early sessions a very young Severiano Ballesteros hit some shots and I told him that he had a lot of talent but that he must change his action or he would develop back trouble. He lifted his right shoulder going back and lifted the left shoulder coming down, classical rock-and-block and reminiscent of Jack Nicklaus.

Many years later he came to me for advice when his tilting style was producing the usual push-fades and the even more destructive snap hooks. In order to replace his tilt of the shoulders with a correct turn, I gave him a drill of making practice swings at an imaginary ball at about hip height. For some years you could see him at tournaments making these flat practice swings whenever he had to wait on a tee.

By the time of the 1993 Ryder Cup match he had reverted to his bad old ways of rocking and blocking and was hitting the ball all over the place. Halfway through the match he asked me for help. He began hitting the ball beautifully on the practice ground but he was so conditioned to the tilting habit that he reverted to type on the course.

He has had an American coach on his case and if this chap can convert Seve into a turner, and make it stick, then the Spanish genius could well be a force in world golf again.

NO PAIN, NO GAIN

These days the pros have mobile fitness centres where they can exercise on weird and wonderful apparatus and keep in trim. If someone had told me as a young man that one day such amenities would be provided at tournaments I would have dismissed the idea as the wildest of fantasies.

My generation was no less concerned with physical fitness and we each had our own ways of conditioning our bodies. Dai Rees, for example, used to train regularly with his beloved Arsenal football club and Max Faulkner was a fitness fanatic who even in his sixties could boast that his waist measurement had not changed since his wartime days as an RAF middleweight boxing champion. Probably the fittest man in the Open Championship field was the American amateur, Frank Stranahan, who travelled everywhere with a full set of bars and lifting weights in his luggage.

I have written elsewhere of my daily routine of long runs with the dog and I also skipped a lot, anything to get me in shape to win the Open. At one time I had to do daily physiotherapy exercises following three operations to strip out varicose veins. I had a steel shoe with a bar inserted from which weights could be hung. I would sit on the bench of the workshop behind my professional's shop and my assistants, David Talbot and others, would have to add the weights, progressively increasing the poundage day by day.

In the end I could straighten my legs with eighty pounds on the shoe. The muscular development was massive. If there really had been anything in the theory that good golf depended on leg-action then I would have been a world beater.

SANDY LYLE

Down the years Britain has produced some wonderful players and Sandy Lyle is a worthy successor to the likes of Harry Vardon and James Braid. Starting with the Boys' Championship, he has had great successes and, thankfully, has remained totally unspoilt by them. Technically he is a bit suspect but there is merit in his taking the club back too much round the right side. This creates a tendency to come over the top but this is a wonderful way of playing golf badly. He stands a little bit open and thumps the ball with an almighty hit down the left side of the fairway, cutting back to the middle.

During the 1988 World Match Play Championship I was working on the new Edinburgh golf course at Wentworth when his caddie came with a request that I take a look at Sandy. To get out of the way we went over to the second tee of the East course and had a good, two-hour session. He was taking the club very much around the right side and not only cutting the ball but, unusually for him, pulling his shots as well.

I teed the ball off the teeing ground, in a position several inches below his feet where the bank made it impossible for him to take the club back on his normal inside line. It had to go straight up as he turned his shoulders. I had to go straight off to Spain that evening and follow his triumphant progress to the title from afar. But when I returned I found waiting for me a typically generous letter of gratitude from this wonderful guy.

These days Sandy is rather more orthodox but I suspect he finds it difficult with his changed technique to know what the ball is going to do and therefore where to aim. The older you get the harder it is to win but Sandy is hitting it pretty well and I would think he has another five good years ahead of him, particularly if he becomes mean about giving shots away when not quite at his best.

SAFETY FIRST

Every good player has a 'safe' shot he can rely on for those occasions when he is facing a particularly narrow fairway, or when the nerves are jangling from the tensions of the moment, or when his regular game is slightly off key. It is invariably a fade, maybe not so long as a normal drive and not so spectacular – but safe.

Tee the ball low. This helps a fade; a high tee tends to promote a hook through hitting early with the hands and rolling the wrists over. Set up to the ball aiming up the left-hand side of the fairway. Open the club-face and hold it open going through the ball, keeping the hands ahead of the club-head. Make sure you turn through as you hit the ball, obviating any independent hand action.

VIVE LA DIFFERENCE

One of my women pupils was an excellent player, four handicap, and on the practice range she would hit a stream of one good shot after another. Inevitably a bad shot would crop up and she would break into tears, absolutely devastated. I tried in vain to console and calm her by saying that she was not in a war. She had no son at the front. Golf was a game and one bad shot did not constitute a disaster. She must keep a sense of proportion.

'But I lack consistency,' she would wail.

All I could reply was: 'If you could eliminate the occasional bad shot you would be the first person ever to do so.'

I like women but I don't pretend to understand them and as a result of failing to crack the secret of the feminine brand of logic I don't feel I have ever been as successful at teaching women as I have with men. With a married couple I may explain something in terms which the man grasps instantly while the wife gives me a look of blank incomprehension.

My wife used to accompany me to golf schools and on one occasion she stood listening to me giving my standard explanation about the swing to a woman pupil. Afterwards Rita said to me: 'That may have sounded all very well to you but it meant nothing to me and, from the look of her, it was all Greek to your pupil as well.'

TODAY'S SLICE

On practice ranges today you see player after player obviously working on an exaggerated in-to-out swing path to cure their slices (without avail, I might add) because they have read or been told that the slice is caused by an out-to-in swing path, as opposed to an open club-face. My remedy is to tee up a ball, set the player square to it and say: 'Now I want you to hit that ball forty-five degrees to the left.' The immediate result is that the player clears his hips and swings from in-back-to-in which squares the club-face and the ball flies straight in spite of his exaggerated feel of an out-to-in swing path.

Arsenic might not be the prescribed cure for arsenical poisoning. But the cure for one man's slice is very often a thought that causes another man's slice. Nearly fifty years ago when I first started to teach golf most slices were out-to-in: right shoulder high and the club-face open at impact. Not so today. More likely the swing is in-to-out with the right shoulder too low, producing a push-fade. The club-face squares when the arc is in-back-to-in.

HOGAN COULD PLAY A BIT

One of the questions put to the *Golf Digest* panel on which I served was: 'How important is it to keep the left wrist straight at the top of the backswing?' The overwhelming consensus of the panelists was that a straight left wrist was indeed a vital necessity so that the downswing could be initiated by the whole of the left side.

I simply had to put forward my minority opinion and did so by asking: 'Do you mean that Ben Hogan did not know how to play golf? Hogan wrote that a cupped left wrist was the secret of a good swing. And what about Roberto de Vicenzo? Or Julius Boros?' Those three examples represented a pretty strong case in favour of cupping the left wrist, as my fellow panelists were forced to concede.

They then asked me if I believed a cupped left wrist was an essential to good golf? The question was an obvious trap. If I said 'Yes' they would bury me under an avalanche of straight-wristed champions, with Jack Nicklaus at the top of the list. In fact, I was never in any danger. I had long since determined that it is quite immaterial whether a golfer has his wrist straight or cupped at the top of the swing, provided the club at that point is aligned parallel to the target line and in the correct plane.

The interesting point to me about that episode was that it illustrated a curious phenomenon in golf, namely the way the doctrine of golf is subject to crazes, like the fashion industry. Many of these crazes have been contradictory. A vogue for playing well within your physical capacity has been superseded by an era of belting the ball with all your might.

There is hardly a part of the body which has not enjoyed a brief spell in the limelight as the key to golf: legs, arms, hips, wrists (both firm and floppy), right big toe, left pinkie, and the chin which, as we have been exhorted at different times, should point to the left of the ball at address and in due season to the right of the ball. In the sixties the stiff left wrist was all the rage, along with square-to-square. For the moment the poor old left wrist has been allowed to retire back into obscurity.

PLAY OR PRACTICE?

There are people who hold the philosophy that golf is golf, and their approach to shots on the practice ground is exactly the same as their attitude and routine for shots on the golf course. Faced with an open expanse of plain turf they will visualise a target and play to it. In order to reproduce the tension of live play they engage in nearest-to-the-pin contests with a companion and bet on themselves.

I agree with modest wagers to concentrate the mind when practising chipping and putting, but when practising full shots, particularly when working to eradicate a fault, a golfer needs to be alone with his thoughts, without distractions.

The whole object of the exercise changes when you go to the practice ground. It does not matter if you hit a bad shot. It may indeed be beneficial. After all, as Bobby Jones pointed out, a golfer learns nothing from his good shots. The practice ground is where a golfer can experiment and learn how to hit the ball high or low, fading or drawing.

On the practice ground it is possible to employ two swing thoughts provided they are in sequence, such as 'Complete the backswing' and 'Hit down and through'. Or 'Watch the club-head contact the ball' and 'Finish high'. When playing on the course I would advocate restricting yourself to one key thought only.

There are, of course, certain universal truths to be observed every time you pick up a club, on the practice ground or out on the course. For example, if you have a good grip don't monkey around with it. And wherever you are and whatever shot you are playing take meticulous care over your routine of aiming the club and setting up to the ball correctly. That way you eliminate the possibility of hitting the vast majority of golf's destructive shots.

WHITE SHOES

Before the war, while Bobby Locke was serving the five-year apprenticeship before becoming eligible for PGA membership, he toured Britain with three friends giving exhibitions and playing challenge matches. The last match of the tour was at Lindrick and before leaving for Liverpool to catch the boat back to South Africa the next day, Bobby made my cousin Jack, the Lindrick pro, get up early for one last round of golf.

When they parted Jack gave Bobby a pair of white golf shoes and a piece of professional advice, namely that he would never do any good in the game until he eliminated his huge hook. Bobby never forgot Jack's kindness and white shoes became an essential element of the golfing uniform he wore for the rest of his life.

When Bobby returned after the war, with the hook more pronounced than ever, incidentally, he requested that Jack play with him in the final practice round before the Open Championship. Bobby won that 1949 Open, of course, so he insisted that Jack play with him in the last practice round before the Open every year thereafter.

I had the pleasure of playing with Bobby many times and found him a most charming and considerate companion. His unvarying golf dress of white cap, white shirt and tie, blue plus-fours, white stockings and shoes was influenced by another and much more significant incident at the 1957 Open Championship. On the final green at St Andrews he marked his ball to the side at the request of his playing companion, Bruce Crampton. In the excitement of the moment Locke forgot to replace his ball in its original position before tapping home the winning putt.

Nobody noticed this lapse at the time but that evening Gerald Micklem was watching TV at his home in Sunningdale and, as a most experienced referee, he could not fail to recognise a breach of golfing procedure. He telephoned the championship committee that evening and an emergency meeting was called to discuss the matter. Locke was questioned and confirmed that he had indeed forgotten to replace his ball. He now had an agonising wait, speculating on whether he might be stripped of his title. The upshot was that the chairman wrote Locke a letter stating that since he had three strokes in hand the committee considered there would be no point in adding two penalty strokes to his score. The result stood and Locke was the true and undoubted champion.

He was so moved by this letter, which became his most prized possession, that he felt he must make some gesture in recognition of the sportsmanship extended to him by the committee. He made no public announcement and he gave no private explanations to anyone, least of all to the Royal & Ancient Golf Club of St Andrews. He himself knew the reason, and that was enough, but from that day hence he never wore plus-fours again. Instead he switched to baggy grey trousers which he wore with the legs rolled half way up his calves.

Someone had once described the portly Locke's stately progress up the fairway as resembling a bishop advancing down the aisle of a cathedral, and Henry Longhurst, who had an eye for social nuances, corrected this picture, remarking that Locke looked more like the bishop's butler. Now, with his trouser legs rolled up, he gave more the appearance of the bishop's butler advancing down the beach for a paddle.

STRAIGHT ENOUGH

The left arm is the radius of the swing arc and it must maintain that radius. To do this it need not be ramrod straight, in the sense that Harry Vardon meant when he said he loved playing against opponents with straight left arms. It must be straight enough without being stiff. In any case, even if the left arm is slightly bent it will be straightened out in the hitting area by centrifugal force.

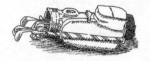

CLIP AND CLEAR

Dave Thomas was an assistant at Moor Park and a player of enormous potential to match his massive size. He was a wonderful driver in particular, hitting the ball vast distances down the left side with just enough fade on the ball to make it leak back into the middle of the fairway.

Since I lived at Moor Park we played a lot together, especially chipping and pitching because he developed a dread of those two strokes. In the natural course of events the technical fault in his action became exacerbated by a mental block with those touch shots. He would putt from forty yards off the green rather than risk making a complete mess of the shot with a lofted club. Dave must be counted as one of my failures.

He never conquered his problem, which was the greatest of pities because, with a reliable short game, he could easily have won the two Open Championships in which he played himself into contention.

His seven-iron at Lytham's seventeenth hole in the 1958 Open was pulled into a greenside bunker because he turned his shoulders from the top instead of starting down with his arms. So by the time the club-head got into the action he was swinging through to the left. In order to get his turn and his downswing back into synch I tried to reverse the order and used to intone a litany on every shot he made: 'Clip it and clear!'

THE SHOP DOESN'T
STOCK SKILL

Back in the mid fifties I was approached by the magazine *Lilliput* to take part in an experiment. They offered me twenty guineas to play a round of golf at my club, Sandy Lodge, using a set of nineteenth-century hickory-shafted clubs and a modern ball. The driver had a forty-six-inch shaft and a tiny head and I remember really having to watch the ball for fear of missing it. The rest of the clubs presented no special problems. The irons consisted of: cleek, driving iron, mid-iron, mashie, spade mashie, mashie niblick and niblick. I went round in seventy-one, more or less the same as I would with my ordinary clubs.

A few weeks later the magazine gave me a box of six new guttie balls and offered me the same fee if I would play a round using my regular steel-shafted clubs and a guttie ball. I unwrapped a couple of the balls and tried them. It was like hitting a stone. By this time the balls must have been thirty or forty years old and had hardened to a degree which invalidated any experiments.

We know, of course, that in the days of the guttie ball the golfers took great pains over storing newly moulded guttie balls and regularly dropping them on to a stone floor to assess from the bounce when they were ready for play. You had to have what they called a good 'stotter'. We could have done that *Lilliput* experiment by moulding new gutties but somebody would have had to rediscover the lost art of judging a good stotter.

Improvements in equipment have clearly played an important part in bringing scores down. The introduction of the rubber-core ball at the beginning of the twentieth century started a chain of improvements which contributed to a steady raising of scoring standards. I'm sure the modern big ball of 1.68-inch diameter goes farther than the small 1.62-inch diameter ball of my youth and without doubt has led to better technique. The manufacturing process of making metal-headed drivers produced clubs which are identical in every detail, a consistency we could never achieve with hand-made wooden heads, just as steel shafts can be matched precisely for weight and flex. Even a master craftsman could not work to such tolerances with hickory and persimmon.

But there is another factor which is of much greater importance in explaining the continuing improvement in golfing standards than advances in the ball or the shaft or the little lump on the bottom end of the shaft. I refer, of course, to the big human lump at the top end of the shaft.

I am not one of those romantics who believe that the crack golfers of yesteryear would have been world-beaters today simply because they had the benefit of using modern equipment. Those old timers believed that the guttie ball called for a higher level of skill than the rubber core. They may have been right at that time. But the world has moved on and I believe that most, if not all of them, would have to practise long and hard to keep up with the stars of today. After all, they did not have that opportunity. Most of their time was spent in earning a living in other ways.

COMMAND
PERFORMANCES

Before the restoration of the Spanish monarchy, King Juan Carlos occasionally dropped in on my teaching sessions and hit balls. He could smash them miles and obviously had the inherent talent to become an accomplished player, but he never took up the game.

Both King Leopold of the Belgians and his son, Prince Baudouin, sent for me to give them lessons, and they would have been automatic choices if the crowned heads of Europe had decided to form a golf team.

I am not so sure about Leopold's wife, Princess Lilian. She had the strongest grip I ever saw and I told her: 'You may be a princess but if you hold the club like that you will always be a hooker.' I could have bitten off my tongue, as the saying goes, when I realised my gaffe. Fortunately, she was unfamiliar with the expression. Either that or she displayed self-control and forbearance of truly regal proportions.

THE EARLY BIRD
CATCHES THE HOOK

Nearly everyone seems to know that the secret of golf, as exemplified by the great players, is something called the late hit. They are not sure exactly what it is, or how to accomplish it, but they want me to give it to them. In fact, most handicap golfers hit too late already. The hand and arm action is delayed because the body has turned through the impact zone too early. They get a slice. If the order is reversed, with the body turning too late, then the result is a hook. There really is no substitute for synchronising the two actions and hitting the ball at the right time, far and true.

JUST DON'T FREEZE

The waggle is an intensely personal ritual and everyone should do something at the address position to ensure that his muscles are relaxed and supple and ready for action. Sam Snead always looked lithe and graceful when he stood to the ball, as if he could, if the mood took him, throw a punch or leap into the air without further preparation. You could always tell when Sam was going to start his backswing because there was a slight hesitation in his final waggle.

The waggle can take various forms. I suppose the commonest one is the inward movement of the right knee immediately prior to the takeaway which has the effect of giving the swing a running start. Two great players of the past, Fred Daly and Arthur Lees, completed the waggle by moving the right foot backwards which also facilitated a smooth takeaway.

A LAW UNTO THEMSELVES

I have a great affection for Ireland – which is a wondrous country for the golfer like myself who also enjoys the country pursuits of shooting and fishing – and for the Irish, who are a wondrous people. For years I had to make at least six visits a year to promote and give lessons at the John Jacobs Golf Centre in the middle of Leopardstown racecourse.

On every trip I experienced some incongruity or little adventure which I felt could only happen in Ireland. For example, I had been working late at the centre and a friend drove me into Dublin for a meal. While he was driving me back to my hotel along a dual carriageway, a car suddenly pulled across our bows at high speed, swerved violently and disappeared down a darkened side street.

My friend, whose quick reactions had saved us from a serious accident, pulled off the main road and followed down the same side street. The driver was attempting a U-turn in the narrow road. My friend leapt from the car, wrenched open the door of the other car, leant in, snatched the keys out of the ignition, threw them over a high wall and returned to resume our journey without uttering a word.

On another occasion Joe Carr took me goose shooting on the famous South Slob at Wexford where we took up our positions in the butts in the pre-dawn darkness. I have to confess for my sins that this was a Sunday morning. Since Joe and I both have competitive natures we had contests and spent an absorbing morning's sport in friendly rivalry. It was not until we broke for lunch that I was able to take due notice of the other six members of the shooting party, now divested of their outer garments. They were all Catholic priests!

MAKE PRACTICE FUN

Nobody has ever mastered the game of golf, or come remotely close to perfection. It is possible to imagine that a great champion will arise who splits every fairway with booming drives and hits his irons with uncanny precision. Some golfers have briefly come so close to that level of control that they could, in the words of Tom Watson, smell total mastery in those areas of the game.

But the greatest of players always have, and always

will have, plenty of scope for improvement in the critical departments of pitching, chipping and putting. These are the skills which offer the best opportunities for saving strokes. Oddly enough, they are commonly the most neglected parts of a golfer's game when it comes to practice. Well, it is not so odd, perhaps, since practising these little touch shots does not give the golfer that tingle of sensuous satisfaction at hitting a full shot flush off the sweet spot. Chipping and putting practice soon gets boring. And if you are bored you do not concentrate properly so the practice does not do you any good.

The answer is to make it competitive. Then it's fun. Then it does you good. When I do team coaching the players are subjected to a tough regime of serious practice followed by a round on the course. But I think they get the most value, and certainly the most enjoyment, from our evening contests.

Each day I mark out tee areas around the practice green for specific holes. The players put their entry money into a hat and play winner-takes-all. The rules are simple. One penalty stroke if your chip does not pitch on to the putting surface and one club and a putter only. I nominate which club must be used. Each day I choose a different club.

With every team, of every nationality, this is the most popular element of the coaching week. I am convinced that it does them the most good. And as a valuable bonus the fierce but friendly competition fosters a wonderful team spirit among players who may have arrived as strangers.

PLAY YOUR
PERCENTAGES

Although when we practise we aim for perfection, even Ben Hogan when he played a record-breaking round reckoned that he hit no more than four or five shots which satisfied one hundred per cent. Golf is a game of misses and the way to win competitions is to hit all your shots no less than about eighty per cent of your potential.

THE SECRET

The golf swing involves two planes, rotation of the body and vertical swinging of the hands and arms. In the backswing, or upswing as it is more aptly termed, the body rotates to the right while the arms swing upwards on a vertical plane. (The body rotation turns the path of the club-head into an inclined plane.)

With some people the upward swing of the hands and arms causes the body to tilt too much into the vertical plane, while others who rotate the body correctly have the arms swinging on a plane which is more useful for beating a carpet draped over a clothes line.

I suppose that what makes golf such a difficult game is synchronising our movements within those two different planes. That is certainly the secret of what we call timing.

NOT SOCIALLY ACCEPTABLE

Ted Dexter was captain of both the cricket and golf teams at Cambridge. I had given him lessons and I was delighted when he invited me to join the Cambridge golf team for a week's coaching at Rye before the 'varsity match. We had a delightful week and Cambridge duly won.

The following year the Oxford team drove to Sandy Lodge and so I was coaching both teams, not nearly so much fun for me because I had to be impartial and partisanship is the very essence of sport.

I coached the Cambridge team again the next year when the 'varsity match was to be held at Royal Lytham and St Annes. When the captain asked the club if I might accompany the team to the match and assist the players, he was informed that the club had its own resident professional and I would not be permitted to attend.

Oddly enough this simply perpetuated a family tradition. My father and George Duncan had two wealthy patrons and the four of them used to go off for golfing weekends during the 1920s, to Le Touquet and other fashionable golfing resorts. When they tried to arrange a game at Lytham they were informed that on no account would the professionals be permitted to enter the clubhouse. The amateurs for their part also declined this privilege.

The Prince of Wales, later to become King Edward VIII, had the same treatment when he took Archie Compston to the Berkshire club for a round of golf. He was told that Archie could not enter the clubhouse, so the Prince also declined that singular honour and departed with Archie and without further ado. The legend persists that the club was thereby stripped of its Royal prefix but that was not the case; it had never been the Royal Berkshire golf club.

PRACTICE SWINGS

Golfers frequently remark: 'If only I could hit the ball with my practice swing.' For purposes of discussion, let us assume that the speaker really does have the perfect practice swing to which he lays claim. It would do him no good to hit the ball with it.

A golf swing is only as good as the position of the club-face at impact. The arc of the swing may be perfect but if the club-face of the driver is more than three degrees off square we miss the fairway. A practice swing is therefore devoid of fear since the squareness (or otherwise) of the club-face at impact is of no account. There is no impact and therefore there is no apprehension.

THE SPIRIT OF GOLF

If you were to ask me to recall an incident which sums up the spirit of golf, and professional golf in particular, my mind would instantly go back to a French Open Championship at La Boulie when the South African Harold Henning needed to finish with two fours to claim second place.

On the seventeenth hole he pushed his drive slightly and the ball ran in among some leaves. He identified the ball by brand name and number, played to the green and holed out. When he retrieved the ball from the hole he looked at it carefully and announced: 'This isn't my ball.' It was indeed the right make, Slazenger B51, and the right number, 3, but he was sure it was not his ball. So he effectively disqualified himself and later went back and found his own ball under the leaves.

Harold's honesty meant that the rest of us all moved up a place in the prize list. On the bus taking the players to the airport we had a whip round and collected virtually the full amount of the second prize and gave it to Harold.

I suppose that the amateur equivalent of this incident would be when Bobby Jones called a penalty stroke on himself for an infringement which nobody saw but him. When someone started to compliment him on his action, Jones brusquely cut him short by saying it was like praising a man for not robbing a bank.

Quite so. I might add that in the French Open incident we were not rewarding Harold for refraining from robbing a bank; we simply felt guilty at profiting from his honesty.

GOLF IS CHILD'S PLAY

The best way for young children to learn golf is not by formal lessons, in my opinion, and certainly not with a full set of clubs. Like most professionals of my generation I learned the rudiments of playing, and competing, for tees, as a boy caddie. We made a little pitch and putt course behind the shop and we had one club, a cut down hickory-shafted mashie, between us. We had beer barrels as barriers so you had to loft the ball and we became remarkably adept and, as is the way at the age, brimming with confidence.

Playing with one club makes you conscious of the club-face and gives you touch and feel. That is how Severiano Ballesteros taught himself how to play and why he has such a magical short game.

As for the full swing, children have a wonderful gift of mimicry and they can acquire a good swing just by copying an accomplished player. In my case we had a two-handicap player at the club and I modelled my action on his. As a great treat I was taken to watch the 1938 Open Championship at Sandwich and I saw Henry Cotton. What a revelation! From then on I modelled myself on Cotton. Every time I played I was Henry Cotton and for a while I even copied the way he walked with the feet pointing straight ahead, or even slightly inwards, a style he had adopted to prevent overswinging and to assist in the current fad of hitting against a braced left side.

He remains among the six finest strikers of a golf ball I have ever seen. They said he couldn't putt. Those who made that rash judgment should have seen him the day many years later at Llandudno where we played each other in a tournament. He absolutely murdered me, of course, and almost every one of his putts went dead into the middle of the hole.

SMALL WORLD

One of the participants in the 1994 Apollo Tour school for new PGA European Tour cardholders, Jonathan Lomas, a very promising young professional, called me to say that he had been going through his grandfather's deed box and had come across a letter from my mother.

The subject matter of that letter took me back to my youth during the early days of the war. I used to help out on the neighbouring farm and the grateful farmer gave me two gilt pigs. Since the fairways were cut by horse-drawn mowers we were able to build a pigsty adjoining the stable.

The Lindrick clubhouse was converted into a maternity home during the war and my mother did the catering. She kept the golf going at weekends by providing snacks in the professional's shop and fed the pigs on the scraps from both establishments. Those two pigs had several litters and so, in the food shortages of wartime, the pig breeding became a useful and thriving little sideline.

That letter concerned the sale of the last of the pigs to Jonathan Lomas's grandfather, the local butcher.

DO NOT EXCEED
THE DOSE

A patient may well receive benefit from a slug of medicinal brandy. One slug, that is. But five slugs? Or six? Well, we all know that he will develop a host of new symptoms. The same goes for golf instruction. The pupil is given a piece of remedial advice such as, let us say, to firm up the grip of his right hand. He is delighted with the improvement in his game. But now he reasons that if he tightens the grip even more he must surely benefit from a proportional further improvement. What actually happens, of course, is that suddenly his swing seizes up and he can't hit his hat. That is when he rings up his teacher in a state of desperation.

You might imagine that a teacher cannot do very much over the telephone. Far from it. I get calls from pupils all over the world, often at most inconvenient times I might add. I am also stopped in the street, or approached in airports by golfers who are in despair over their games. I do not mind and I can give an assurance that it is not necessary at all to see them swing a club in order to suggest a remedy.

The requests for help that do raise my blood pressure a little are the ones which start: 'You must help me. I think I'm getting across the line at the top and that's making me come into the ball all askew and as a result I spend most of my time looking for the ball in the rough.'

My reply to this type of call can get slightly testy, especially if the caller is in a different time zone and has been inconsiderate enough to overlook the fact that for me it is two o'clock in the morning: 'Don't start telling me what you think you are doing. Tell me what the ball is doing. Specifically describe the flight of the ball from the driver, from the long irons, from the mid-irons and from the short irons.' Armed with that information I can easily deduce how the club-face is being presented to the ball. That is the key and I can now make a diagnosis and offer a remedy, particularly if I happen to be familiar with the enquirer's swing.

At the end of most lessons with pupils who, because of the distances involved, are not able to be taught often, I invite them to phone me (first making sure there is no football/boxing/golf on TV), and if they will tell me what the ball is doing I can be of real help.

The most common situation is that after a while the pupil reverts to the original mistake. Only in a few cases does the instruction become exaggerated.

YOU BOUNDER, SIR;
YOU'VE DEFILED
MY LADY WIFE!

I feel sure it is true of all golf coaches that teaching is more, much more, than just a way of making a living. The rewards of having a former pupil come up to you and say how their golf, and their lives, were transformed by the help you gave them many years before is, literally, beyond price. The satisfaction of giving someone the source of one of life's great pleasures is the stimulus which keeps me teaching long after I should have retired to the river bank with my trout rod.

Very often, however, the ex-pupil who has poured out his gratitude for giving him a lifetime of happiness on the links then hits me with the whammy of a codicil: 'But you have absolutely ruined my wife's swing.'

That, I must say, is hard to take since never in my entire life have I even met the lady in question. What has happened in almost all cases, of course, is that in teaching the man and explaining in patient detail how the swing operates, you create the monster of a self-appointed golf professional who goes home and gives his wife lessons. He may have come to me as a tilter with an unduly upright swing arc which, in due course, I have put right. But you can imagine the havoc he would create if he applied my swing-flatter remedy to a wife whose swing was already excessively flat.

To the best of my knowledge Alexander Pope did not spend a lot of time on the practice ground curing the slices of seventeenth century golfing tyros but he certainly said it for all golf teachers when he wrote: 'A little learning is a dangerous thing . . .'

NEVER GIVE UP

Early in my career I was playing in a competition and soon into the round I suffered a disaster that cost me four or five strokes. It was a real body blow and completely knocked the stuffing out of me, to the extent that for the rest of the round I was just going through the motions. I stopped competing and, my goodness, how the strokes mounted up. In retrospect that was not such a disaster because it taught me a valuable lesson. As Bobby Jones remarked with his customary sagacity: you learn only from your mistakes.

When I am trying to impress on professional golfers the importance of trying your utmost on every shot I remind them that almost always the winner will have had at least two disasters in his four rounds.

The most salutory example I have ever witnessed of the virtue of trying on every shot was Jack Nicklaus in the first round of the Open Championship at Sandwich in 1981. On the eve of the championship he had received word of his son Stevie's car accident and with his mind in a turmoil of worry he was hitting the ball very badly by his standards in the dreadful conditions of wind and rain in that opening round.

I had gone back to my hotel and watched in fascination at the drama on TV. He was on the thirteenth hole and at that point was about twelve over par. But he was not giving up; he was obviously trying his very hardest on every stroke and scrambling magnificently. I think he got up and down four times to restrict his score to eighty-three.

The next day, after reassuring news from home, he played a fine round of sixty-six and just made the cut, which he would not have done if he had packed it in the previous day. That was a wonderful lesson from the greatest competitor there has ever been.

DIFFERENT GAME, SAME MADNESS

Many athletes from different sports choose golf as their favourite recreation but for some reason I cannot explain, cricketers seem to have a special affinity for the game. Perhaps it is just that I am more aware of golfing cricketers because of my own passion for cricket in all its forms, but most especially for the game in its highest expression, as played by Yorkshire County Cricket Club.

I have been a cricket fanatic ever since I opened the bowling for my school as a gangling six-footer at the age of fifteen. When I had my golf centre at Sandown Park two of my regular customers were the cricketing twins, Eric and Alec Bedser. I had a deal with them. I would teach them golf for half an hour in exchange for them sitting down with me afterwards and talking cricket for half an hour.

One of my good friends was Leonard Crawley, a crack shot and an international-class cricketer and golfer. He once faced the exquisite dilemma of having to choose whether to accept Douglas Jardine's invitation to join the English Test team for what was to become the bodyline tour of Australia, or to join the British and Irish team which was due to sail to Boston for the Walker Cup match. He chose the latter. Leonard, who was to become the golf correspondent of the *Daily Telegraph*, was a ferocious batsman of whom one disillusioned bowler once remarked: 'The only way to bowl at Leonard is to release the ball and then duck for safety behind the umpire.'

On one occasion I had to follow Leonard as speaker at a golfing dinner and he entertained the audience with a series of anecdotes at my expense, mostly to do with Yorkshire cricket. For once I was ready with a counter-attack because my Bible at that time was Herbert Sutcliffe's book, *For England and Yorkshire*, and I well knew that the record opening stand of 555 had been compiled by Yorkshire, of course, by Sutcliffe and Percy Holmes, at Leyton, against Essex, and that the captain of Essex on that historic occasion was none other than Leonard Crawley.

I in turn, was on the receiving end of an elegant counter-punch from a great golfer, and great friend, who once scored a century in a guest appearance for Kent and then mesmerised the opposition with his legspin bowling. I refer, if you have not already guessed, to Peter Thomson.

The year he won one of his five Open Championships in the fifties the English cricket tourists won the first

Test in Australia and I cabled Thomson: 'We may not be much good at golf but we sure can play cricket.'

There was no response until, in due season, Australia crushed England in the second Test. The cable read: 'As you were saying . . .'

AN OBVIOUS CHAMPION

I was working in Cairo when Peter Thomson broke his journey there on his first trip to Britain. The flight from Australia took two days in the lumbering Constellations and, even as a lithe eighteen-year-old, he was extremely stiff when he disembarked. He was travelling with Norman von Nida and they had to go straight to the golf course to play an exhibition match against me and Hassan Hassanein.

Thomson's game immediately caught my attention because of his touch with the short shots. His stiff back meant that his long game was wayward but he scrambled to telling effect, getting the ball up and down so regularly that he reached the turn in par-thirty-six. By now the hot sun and the exercise had done their remedial work on his back and he turned on a dazzling display of shot-making. If it had been possible to buy shares in that teenager I would have invested every penny I could scrape together.

FROM GOOD TO GREAT

It says a lot about the inner drive of the true champions that even when they are enjoying great success, making pots of money and winning tournaments, they are prepared to jump off the gravy train and work for months on end to improve their technique.

The first example that comes to mind is Byron Nelson. I first met him in 1955 when I played in the old Thunderbird Classic and he invited me to join him in a practice round. What a player! He made me feel like a fifteen-handicapper. I did not have an opportunity to talk with him again until 1967 when we were both doing television commentaries on the Open Championship at Hoylake.

I used positively to devour instruction books in those days, any golf books come to that, and I had read his book. So I commented that when he started out he must have swung the club in a very flat arc. He concurred that this was indeed the case. He made that flat swing work well enough to win tournaments but he was not consistent. He would win a tournament and the next week he would fail to qualify. So he took three months off and changed his grip, removing two of his three knuckles from his view, and working on taking the club straight back and up.

Having grooved his adjusted swing he made a statement that, for a man of such inherent humility, bordered on providence-tempting arrogance: 'I believed I would never play badly again.' But that was about the size of it. He never did.

In his first instruction book, *Power Golf*, Ben Hogan advocated a three-knuckle grip and that is how he played. In my conversation with Nelson I remarked that it had taken a serious car accident to force Hogan to change his grip. Nelson corrected me. He said that Hogan had been practising with a weak left-hand grip before the accident – Henry Cotton said that it was he who had convinced Hogan of the need for such a change – but that when he got out on the course Hogan reverted to his familiar three-knuckle grip.

Having read *Power Golf* I had been very anxious to watch Hogan and I had my opportunity at the 1953 Open Championship at Carnoustie. His grip was completely different from the illustrations in the book. Hogan's enforced lay-off produced what was probably the most thorough and effective revision of a golf swing of them all.

Roberto de Vicenzo, that lovely, self-deprecating character with his infectious good humour and fractured English, was another player who realised that he could never achieve his full potential until he eliminated a fault. His left hand was too far over the top of the club and it took him six months, hitting a thousand balls a day, to get comfortable with his new grip. Then he won the Open Championship and almost won the Masters.

Nick Faldo is the most recent example of a highly successful player withdrawing from competitive play to rebuild his swing. He was a rocker and he was very fortunate to find in David Leadbetter a teacher so well suited to his needs. It seems to me that Faldo sees golf in terms of infinite complexity whereas I believe and teach that golf, although admittedly a most difficult game, is essentially a simple game. Indeed I might go so far as to say the simpler the better.

Jack Nicklaus never actually withdrew from competitive golf in order to make changes to his swing. But he was a prodigious worker on his golf. He established what is now the standard routine for professional golfers of hitting hundreds of balls a day and also of going straight to the practice ground after a competitive round in order to iron out a fault. For years he struggled, without lasting success, to convert his shoulder tilt into a turn.

One day when I was in his office I was emboldened to remark, using the verbal shorthand of the profession: 'You won most of your titles missing it.'

He grinned and replied: 'Yes, but I'm smarter than the other guys.' And that was no less than the truth of it.

A WASTE OF MY TIME
AND YOUR MONEY

Regrettably too many lessons do not do a scrap of good. I have reached this bleak conclusion after many years of trying to help golfers who come to me with deeply engrained bad habits. With this type of pupil it is easy enough to get them hitting shots which are an absolute revelation. I can show them their potential for hitting shots which are beyond their wildest ambitions. But bad habits die hard and unless the pupil is prepared to work long and hard on the practice ground the bad habit will reassert itself.

These days when, for example, a habitual slicer seeks

help I often start by asking how much time and effort he is prepared to put into the physiotherapy exercises after I have rebroken the bone of his bad habit and set it straight. If he says that he really cannot spare the time to practise much, which is the case for many people, I tell him: 'Then go on the way you are now and simply aim off to allow for your slice.'

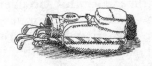

QUICK FIXES

If you are having problems with your game, do not ask your twenty-four-handicap companion what you are doing wrong. He does not know; if he did know he would not be twenty-four-handicap. Besides, you have an absolutely reliable informant at hand, ready and willing to give you a precise analysis of your fault. Always remember: the flight of the ball tells it all. So observe first the direction the ball takes immediately it leaves the club-face.

If it goes in a straight line out to the right, and then continues on that same straight flight path without deviating right or left, that is a *push*, which is caused by swinging the club-head on an in-to-out path with the club-face square to that swing arc. This is the result of standing with the shoulders closed at the address and playing the ball too far back in the stance. *Remedy:* open the stance, move the ball forward and concentrate on turning through the shot to give you the required in-to-square-to-in swing path.

Frequently the *push* is accompanied by a *hook*. The

ball starts off going straight to the right and then bends to the left. *Remedy:* if the ball swerves to the left you adjust your grip by rotating it to the left, that is in an anti-clockwise direction as you look down on it. Now combine your new grip with the *push* remedy.

The ball that starts straight left and continues without swerving left or right is a *pull*, the result of an out-to-in swing path and a square club-face, caused by an open stance and the ball too far forward in the stance. *Remedy:* square the shoulders at address, move the ball back in the stance and concentrate on swinging from the inside.

Again, the *pull* is often associated with a sideways movement as the speed drops and side spin takes effect. If the flight pattern is a bend to the right, that tells you that the club-face was open at impact. *Remedy:* adjust your grip by rotating the hands to the right, or clockwise, and combine your new grip with the *pull* remedy. We have already covered how to adjust the grip if the ball bends to the left. Remember that golden rule: if the ball bends to the left, adjust your grip round to the left; if the ball bends to the right, adjust your grip round to the right.

If the ball goes like a rocket straight up the right centre of the fairway and then as it begins to descend it tails away slightly to the left, then what you have is a pure *draw*. There is no *remedy* required because there is no fault. This is the natural shape of a good shot so leave well alone and cherish it.

The ball that won't get airborne is what is called a *thin* shot. It is caused by turning the shoulders from the top of the backswing without simultaneously swinging down with the arms and hands. The diagnosis self-evidently supplies the *remedy:* bring your arms into the action.

Conversely, hitting behind the ball, or a *fat* shot, is caused by swinging the arms independently without the necessary body action. *Remedy:* turn away and turn back as you swing up and swing down.

Hitting off the *heel* of the club is caused by too flat a swing plane from an open stance. *Remedy:* close the shoulders and swing up and under, concentrating on hand and arm action. Practice with the ball positioned below the level of your feet.

Shots off the *toe* of the club are caused by lifting the club straight up. *Remedy:* stand with a good, upright posture, swing the club-head back away from the ball by turning and feel that you are making a flat swing. Practise with the ball above the level of your feet and concentrate on body action.

If you are having trouble with the little chip and pitch shots you can make a dramatic improvement with a simple experiment. Try playing these shots with a shorter backswing than normal and then with a longer backswing. One or other of these variations may well do the trick. And always finish those strokes with the club-head close to the ground.

BY ROYAL COMMAND

I was preparing for one of my regular coaching sessions with the German teams when I received word that, since the February weather in Spain, where we customarily held our sessions, had been disappointing in recent years, they had switched to Morocco. I flew out a day early and when I reported to the Royal Dar Es Salaam club at Rabat I was immediately invited to join the sister of King Hassan II for a game of golf.

The next day I was busy with my tutorial duties on the practice ground when a senior government official approached and informed me that I must make myself available every afternoon to play golf with His Majesty. My expression must have conveyed some hint of my unspoken thoughts because the official made it eminently clear that Morocco's continued welcome to myself and the German teams was dependent upon my embracing this signal honour without demur.

Arrangements were quickly made for the German teams to be suitably looked after during my enforced afternoon absences. My services were not required every day but when we did play, on the King's private nine-hole course within the grounds of his royal palace – one of several such courses around the country, I might add – the experience was quite fantastic, using that over-worked word in its literal sense of dreamlike fantasy.

His Majesty started by entering a small tent and making his choice from a selection of some thirty pairs of golf shoes on display. A truck containing twenty sets of golf clubs followed our progress around the course. The King is a great enthusiast for the game and a fair striker of the ball but it is difficult to assess his handicap level. His golfing companions perforce are drawn from the ranks of ministers, diplomats and high government officials, all men with an acute appreciation of which side their bread is buttered and, accordingly, most generous ideas of what constitutes a royal gimme. There is, in short, no such thing for the King as a second putt in this school.

The King is a wizard out of the rough, a fact not entirely unconnected with the retinue of some fifty or sixty solicitous attendants: security men, flunkeys, functionaries, forecaddies and the like. They made sure his ball was always nicely teed up. I am sure that the King does not command such favourable consideration. He would surely get more genuine satisfaction from his golf if he played in a hard-nosed fourball which insisted on seeing every putt into the hole and no hanky panky in the rough. But being who he is, his is the only form of golf available to him.

Urgent affairs of State dictated how many holes the King played. When the game stopped and the King departed, we all adjourned to a large marquee in the grounds. Here were served mountains of couscous, whole roasted sheep, barons of beef, pigeon pies, a profusion of fruits, and steaming hot mint tea served from silver pitchers.

One corner of the tent was set aside especially for the visiting English *professeur de golf*. I had to make do with caviar and Veuve Cliquot.

MUFFLE THE MOANERS

The first year I taught the German squads, male and female, senior and junior, there was one young man whose abominable behaviour threatened to ruin the entire seminar. Nothing was right for him. He complained incessantly as a matter of habit. Something had to be done about him. But what?

One evening at dinner I put this question to Thomas Hubner, the current German amateur champion and a very decent guy. After some thought he came up with the bright idea of forming a Non-muffling Society, muffling being the German equivalent of whingeing or moaning. An inaugural meeting was held, officers were appointed and the aims and objects of the society were defined in the constitution in the form of a simple resolution never to muffle.

So right from the start of my association with the German squads muffling was strictly *verboten* and as a result the five or six years I spent coaching them were most enjoyable for me. The anti-muffling campaign created a friendly and positive spirit among the players and as a consequence the teaching process was much more effective. The women's team were runners-up in Europe during that period, thanks in some degree, I am sure, to the *esprit de corps* generated by their determination to get on with the job without muffling. There is a lesson in there for all golfers: you will never become a great golfer if you constantly muffle about bad lies, the weather, poor clubs or whatever.

IN-TO-STRAIGHT

If the putter shaft were fitted absolutely at right angles to the club-head, and I am talking about conventional putters, not those fancy broom-handle jobs, we could take the club straight back and straight through with a perfect pendulum stroke. But the rules say that the shaft has to be set at an angle and we must accommodate that angle by taking the club-head back slightly on an inside arc. The return swing is from in-to-straight through the ball.

The chip is exactly the same except that you hit slightly down on the ball. To achieve this at the address the hands and weight favour the left side. Swing the club predominantly with the hands and arms while allowing the body to move in sympathy.

BERNARD GALLACHER

I first taught Bernard Gallacher at Largs when he was a member of the Scottish junior team. At that time, if he'd had fifty knuckles he would have shown all of them. I managed to cut him down to four or so, but he was my favourite type of pupil because he never accepted anything I told him at face value. He wanted to know all the whys and wherefores and I had to prove everything by demonstration before he would take it on board. He was then, and always remained, the fiercest competitor I have ever known as well as being a superb player on his day, such as the time he beat Lee Trevino in the 1969 Ryder Cup match. I was doing TV commentaries when he successfully defended his Dunlop Masters title, and we chatted each evening. If he had hit a bad shot he would tell me: 'Don't worry, John, I shan't do that tomorrow.'

In the early days he had a very rounded, flattish swing which gave him a pronounced draw. His action was totally repetitive and he had a wonderful short game. One day he rang and asked if I would take a look at him. When he arrived at my Sandown Park Golf Centre I was horrified. Someone had told him, rightly enough so far as it went, that he needed to be more upright. His swing, that is the arc of his hands, arms and club, would have benefited from being more upright but he had become a rocker and blocker. His turn had gone; his right side was lifting, causing him to come over the top and cut everything. He had got it all wrong for quite a long time and, although he now is a fine orthodox hitter (certainly in practice), he never fully regained the confidence he had as a boy.

Bernard and his wife Lesley have been good friends to me. I attend dinners at Wentworth fairly regularly and they kindly give me a bed to avoid the drink-and-drive problem. These days we play three or four times a year and when I take a look at his swing he invariably hits the ball wonderfully well. He can certainly play well enough to add to his tally of tournament victories, but his response to any such suggestion is that he can hit it well enough when he is playing with me but he can't do it when the gun goes, so very different from his attitude in his younger days.

Of course he is tremendously busy as head professional at the Wentworth Club and deeply involved with affairs of the PGA European Tour. He cannot do justice to his own game. I had the same problem at Sandy Lodge and from time to time I needed to get away from the intensive daily routine of teaching. Playing tournaments was for me the change that was as good as a rest. I do wish Bernard could do the same and enjoy a swan-song to his fine career by adding one or two more titles to it before he packs it in. Better still if he were to captain a winning Ryder Cup team.

TIGER WOODS

The American golfing public has been waiting, with an increasing sense of anxiety and frustration, for a new superstar and, on the evidence of a fabulous amateur career, high hopes have been pinned on the stout shoulders of Tiger Woods.

I have been asked whether I think those hopes are justified and I just don't know. For one thing, and it is a pretty important prerequisite for judging a golfer's potential, I have never seen him swing a club. But even if I had studied his technique and observed his demeanour and tactical judgment on the course, I would still be unable to make a confident assessment of his potential. I have seen so many young prodigies, whom everybody raves about and proclaims as future champions, only to be proved quite wrong.

On a recent coaching visit to Spain I saw a class of twelve boys, aged from ten to fourteen, who were all between scratch and three-handicap. On the evidence of how well they hit the ball you would be tempted to assert that they were all bound to become champions. I would say that José Maria Olazabal was no better than that class of boys when he was their age.

Spain now has a nucleus of very good teachers and those boys, all from the same school, have an excellent coach. They are probably getting a better golfing education than could be obtained at many American universities, where some of the professionals – I do not say all of them, by any means – are not teachers; they merely organise the golf programme. But it is too early to attempt a judgment, of Tiger Woods or that class of Spanish boys. It is plain enough for all to see that they have good swings, but golf is more, much more, than that and judgment must be reserved until golfers are competing at senior level, against strong and experienced opposition. Only then can you discern a player's ability to compete, his steadfastness, his patience, his strength of purpose and all the other qualities which make up the temperament of a champion.

You may ask what manner of expert I think I am, since anybody can say: 'Wait and see.' Believe me, it is because of my experience and professional knowledge that I insist that no prognosis can be made until all the symptoms have revealed themselves. So, yes: we shall just have to wait and see.

IAN WOOSNAM

For me Ian Woosnam swings the club exactly the way I think it should be swung. We are all astonished at the distances he hits the ball but, as he turns his shoulders and swings the club up at the same time, he is the perfect exemplar of the secret of long hitting: club-head speed *correctly applied.* Nobody applies it more correctly. It seems to me sometimes that his temperament is affected by the way he is putting but he is the model for every young player to copy in terms of technique. He is a better Hogan, if you like – more fluid and more correct in that he does not have to drive it through and hit as late as Hogan did.

ERNIE ELS

This strapping young South African seems to have absolutely everything. The putts he holed getting himself into a play-off for the U.S. Open in 1994, and then the putts he holed during the play-off, told us all we needed to know about the quality of his temperament. As for his technique, it is unflawed. Like every good player, his swing gives him a natural draw. Many such players – and I was one of them – switched to a fade in the course of time as an antidote to a possible hook.

He is immensely strong and in the years to come he may cut back on the power and switch to more of a ball-control policy. Of course I could be wrong and he might continue to accept the risk of an occasional penalty and go on giving the ball the full treatment, a bit like Roberto de Vicenzo. Either way, he is a terrific prospect.

NICK PRICE

We have discussed earlier how the elements in the making of a champion are to start with the right temperament, acquire the right technique and then work on physical strength. I have not talked about golf with Nick but you get to learn a lot about a person from watching him play and I suspect that he did not have the temperament for tournament golf when he started. But he acquired a quite superb technique, so effective that he won in spite of his temperament. And through the experience of winning he developed the champion's temperament.

Now he has got it all. I do not think he is particularly strong physically but his impact is so good that he is pretty long. What a lovely person and, like Sandy Lyle, an absolute gentleman.

VILE CUSTOMS

On one of my course-building trips to Pakistan I enjoyed an excellent day's partridge shooting and my host, the

C-in-C of the Pakistan Air Force and also the chairman of Pakistan International Airways, asked me if I would like to take some of the birds home with me. I remarked that it was surely illegal to import them. Not at all, he replied, provided you have the proper paperwork. He duly provided me with the necessary certification that the birds had been properly refrigerated and were free of disease and so when the customs officer at London Airport pursed his lips and said, 'No, no. You can't bring them in,' I replied, 'Yes, yes. Indeed I can,' and produced the documentation.

Off he went to confer with higher authority and returned with a shamefaced grin and said: 'You are quite right. Everything is in order.' I departed with my partridges and the special satisfaction which comes from scoring a victory, albeit a small one, over the forces of bureaucracy.

A year later I received a note from HM Customs, London Airport, which read: 'We have today destroyed a consignment of twenty-four partridges from Pakistan addressed to you.' It was too late to protest or argue the toss. All I could do was ruefully reflect that you can't win 'em all.

SMART BOY

One of the members at Gezira Sporting Club was a Turkish prince, Jemal el Din, and he loved to hit balls on the practice range. Everyone used their own practice balls in those days and the boy caddie who picked up the balls for the prince used to get an extra tip whenever his master belted out a really long drive which reached the end of the range. This resourceful little chap perfected the technique, for use whenever the prince hit a longish one, of dancing with delight and then picking up the ball between his toes as he ran to the end of the field where he would pick up the ball and hold it aloft with shouts of excited congratulation.

A NIGHT TO REMEMBER

I shall never forget Christmas Eve of 1949 during my time as the professional at Gezira Sporting Club. Rita and I drove out to the pyramids at Giza on a clear, starlit night. Flares had been lit under the Sphinx and the flames reflecting on the rock seemed to bring that mythical beast to life. There were very few people around and we just sat and enjoyed the balmy night air and the magical scene. And then, quite by chance, an Arab riding a donkey appeared out of the darkness and walked across our field of fire-lit vision and disappeared into darkness again. We did not speak. Communication at that moment did not require words.